The Theory of Mind Revolution

By

Bernard Aleman

For My Aubree.
For My Zaelynn.

June 11, 2015, 1:40PM

"My honest feedback on your work is that it has little potential to be a book. I do think you have a gift for writing…. But the main problem is that your entire premise is based on mostly incorrect conjecture, not scholarly content backed up by evidence. Unless you're an anthropologist, your thoughts on these matters belong in a conversation amongst friends, not in print. Of course, there is room in the world for people's opinions -- usually on blogs or on talk shows though."
                    -A Published Author-

Wow…harsh; however, she was, and still is, accurate. The following IS conjecture. It is conjecture painted as nothing more than the observations of someone who is no: anthropologist, theologian, historian, scholar, clinician, scientist, or expert.

As to whether or not it is "incorrect", well…
                    -B. Aleman-

-Prologue-

This morning I woke up and turned on the television. Some news channel was running the latest right-now atrocity of the planet. *Benazir Bhutto...the former Prime Minister of Pakistan was killed today...she was shot in the neck and in the chest...her assailant then blew himself up...killing 140 people...*

The news channel did not air video of the assassination or the ensuing murders. Instead it played footage of events taking place hours later. Ms. Bhutto's flag-draped casket was shown floating upon a sea of upturned hands as mourners carried her over an undulating ocean of grief stricken people. The pictures were powerful. I imagine in scenes like this they always have been. Time and place in history have made no difference as to how people react when a person on whom they have chosen to bestow their hope and faith is cut down before that person's potential for good is realized. Shock is followed by sadness and sadness is always, always followed by anger.

It is a fact there exist a very real and profound courses of emotions people must endure whenever they are met with such personal adversity or tragedy. The nature of the adversity or tragedy will dictate the weight and direction of the emotional course to be taken and because every situation and every individual is different then there is no concrete rhyme or reason as to how any one will behave with their regard. Save for in one instance.

Only in cases where a beloved and influential leader of the people has been unjustly taken might one be able to correctly predict, and not be surprised by, the collective behavior elicited from such an event. Of course all emotions will be attached to such an occurrence. There will be pain and grief in the forms of sorrow and fear and denial and anger and rage. Of these, two will be felt more intensely than the rest. They will be anger and they will be rage. There is a very profound reason for this and it has been with us since our beginning.

Humans, like all other animals, inherently know Good from Bad. It is why that particular anger and that particular rage, in events such as the aforementioned, will always be easily predicted. At our deepest core we know and truly understand the essentialities of life. At our deepest core we know it is better to co-exist and to cooperate than not. At our deepest core we know it is better to fight only when there is no other option. At our deepest core we know killing another may only be warranted when it is for the sake of truly defending our lives or the lives of those whom we have been entrusted to protect. At our deepest core we absolutely hold these Three Truths to be self-evident.

This is why the severe collective pain and grief that comes as a direct result of a beloved and influential leader of the people having their life ripped from their skin gives birth to such intense anger and rage which in turn makes that collective reaction so pure and complete and visceral; as in the observed reactions by the people of Pakistan after the assassination of Ms. Bhutto.

One need only look into the mirrors of history to see how honest these observations are. Our collective human history is wrought full of instances wherein people have been summarily robbed of their hope and faith through the arrow, dagger, sword ,bullet or bomb by those who did not wish to see the dawning of a new and better age. Lincoln murdered. Crazy Horse murdered. Zapata murdered. Gandhi murdered. Evers murdered. JFK murdered. MLK murdered. RFK murdered. X murdered. Guevara murdered. Bhutto …murdered.

Of course this is but a very, very condensed list of some of the most well-known and influential leaders of people who met their untimely ends by cruel and violent means, but it serves to underscore the one crucial point that we, as human animals, feel ALL the ugliness and despair of humanity's loss in each of these cases because we so absolutely and inherently know Good from Bad.

We feel the powerful weight of their gravity because they are a knowledge that is founded and grounded in pure and natural instinct. It is an instinct of the most primitive sort from which we were never meant to be separated for this was, and still is, how Life ensured the human animal would remain connected to all others in more than just an institutionally superficial manner.

But, this is not how we behave. At this point in our history we have become something else almost entirely. The human animal is set apart from all other creatures. It is "better" than the "lower" and "lesser" animals of this world. The human animal asserts this is so because it is intelligent and capable of in-depth reasoning therefore making its continued existence not just a mere bi-product of being dependent upon sheer instinct.

The human animal is set apart because unlike the "lower" and "lesser" life forms it shares this blue and green planet with it uses its self- ingratiating powers of intelligence and reasoning to justify its collective actions or the lack thereof. It tells itself these collective actions and/or non-actions are for its or the greater good's benefit, but ironically these calculated proceedings are more often than not to its own or the greater good's detriment.

The result of this unabashed intelli-reasoning, if you will, is the repeated and voluntary foregoing of the human animal's purest instincts; carried out to such a disquieting extent that it has convinced itself this particular *modus operandi* is what has always been the natural course of its evolutionary progression throughout time and history.

The human animal is the most transparent form of contradiction personified. It sees and knows all, or so it proclaims, save for the blatant and disrespectful manner in which it chooses to ignore nature's very simple and very effective formula for Life; The Three Truths: At our deepest core we know it is better to co-exist and to cooperate than not. At our deepest core we know it is better to fight only when it is absolutely necessary. At our deepest core we know killing another may only be warranted when it is for the sake of truly defending our lives or the lives of those whom we have been entrusted to protect. The human animal has chosen to deny its instincts...it is guilty of hubris and it is guilty of blasphemy... to their highest degrees.

Something happened over the course of the human animal's collective progression and it made it easy for us today to effortlessly dismiss The Three Truths we hold to be self-evident. It happened in a proverbial wink of the eye. This event would change the world. It would change us and it would set the stage for what would happen next.

Through this event we arrived at a point wherein we recognized the potentiality of our intelligence. We initiated an age of grand achievement, but in an incredibly ironic twist were eventually led to act on a stage of accepted and continued mediocrity. Then we reasoned our instincts away.

In doing this we sabotaged the simple formula Life had set forth for us. We muddled our existence with unnecessary and arrogant complexities and because this was so we have all been responsible in one way, shape, or form for the continued de-evolution of our many civilizations to some extent or another from that point hence.

Around our contemporary world as members of various "civilized" societies we collectively behave in much of the same ways. Every day we wander through our lives thinking largely of our selves. We worry about this and fret about that all the while cursing what little opportunities are thrown our way. Whatever we have is never enough. We work harder and longer so that we can have more money with which to buy more and more stuff so that we can ultimately end up broke again. We drive bigger and faster cars and live in bigger and bigger houses so that our children might have to dig us out of debt even after we have ironically been put in the ground. Everything bad is always someone else's fault because we, after all, are simply trying to survive.

Our governments are even more complicit in the continued de-evolutions of our civilizations. Corrupting government, I have heard it said, is the world's third oldest profession. By far the most severe consequence of all of these behaviors is a general sense of acceptable apathy toward our fellow human. These are merely some examples of how we have managed to alter Life's simplicity and set the stage for the emergence and continuation of the uncaring world in which we have lived for far too long.

We humans are absolutely exceptional beings. There is a capacity within the innermost reaches of our souls to be capable of the most honorable actions ever witnessed. We have conquered the skies and have flown to the moon. We have conquered the crossing of the seas. We have built everlasting civilizations so that our progeny might never forget those who came before them. Yes, humans are quite exceptional. Unfortunately, our skill and desire for creation is matched step for step with our skill and talent for absolute destruction.

In every corner of the world on any given day there is always something horrifically awesome occurring. People are dying of starvation and neglect. They are fleeing wars and being displaced into lands that cannot sustain their numbers. They are being ruthlessly butchered. They are being sold as slaves and abused/ tortured in nefariously creative ways. Rain forests are being murdered. Wild habitats are being stolen and raped. The air is becoming toxic. Our polar ice caps are melting.

We are all aware of this. Most of us simply ignore these evil happenings of the world. The rest of us pretend to care and then find reasons to convince ourselves there is nothing we can do. We tell ourselves the odds are too overwhelming to even try. And so we do not.

Once upon a time the world was a more quiet and caring place. Perhaps it was because people as a whole consciously lived among one another and not just amongst each other. This has not been the case for a very long time. One need only look at the many states of egregiousness in existence throughout the world today to know this is true. Maybe there are many reasons for this. Maybe there are none. I believe there is just one and it has spoiled our collective consciousness of existence. I believe we have forsaken the essence of our female human animal and she has forgotten who she has always been. She has been tricked, manipulated, and coerced into relinquishing her power so that men could rule the world.

-On The Young Humans-

Long ago when the human animal was young and the Earth was already very old nature's simple formula for Life existed holistically. It lived everywhere and in everything. That which Life had intended for all the inhabitants of this blue and green planet to be was easy to see. There was co-exist and cooperate. There was fight only when absolutely necessary. And there was kill only when truly defending your life or the lives of those whom you had been entrusted to protect. In the beginning there were only The Three Truths; nothing more...nothing less. In the beginning it was perfect.

Throughout the age of stone the human animal was beautifully primitive. It constructed and hunted utilizing only the most rudimentary of tools. It sheltered in caves. It is almost certain that it communicated with a language (or languages) of sorts; spoken or perhaps not...perhaps both. It is wondrous to think about what must have been the instinctual simplicity of Life; food and shelter and the survival of the species. Life was true and honest and unrelenting. It was everything except complex. But above all it was fair and just. As such the natural order of things was in place and the world was quiet and good.

With the world and Life existing as one in a profoundly sound state of equilibrium it is not difficult to surmise the behavior of the human animal was likely not very different to that of the other animals with which it was running around on this blue and green planet in that day and age. This in short was due to the fact that The Three Truths applied to, and worked for, all in the same perfect way.

Such as the world was then one may be able to clearly grasp just what the human animal's primary motivations were for adhering to Life's simple formula. Life must continue therefore: One must eat, one must be protected, and one must pro-create. The human animal was in essence more like all the other creatures of that once-upon-a-time earth.

Hence, logic commands that since the animal kingdom of today is perhaps exactly what it was in that once-upon-a-time, it is almost certain there continues to exist a mirror of historical reference to substantiate this observation. That mirror lives within the behaviors of all of those creatures many of us continue to insist are *lower* and *lesser* than we.

In the case of the human animal there is one very crucial element to this argument and it is founded upon the manner in which females and males behave in concert. It is in the behaviors exhibited by females and males with regard to mating that we can begin to clearly understand just how and why the world has devolved into the state of seemingly endless sad affairs it is today from the pure and balanced realm it once was.

When observing our contemporary animal kingdom there are two very distinctive, but significantly important things which stand out more prominently than all else. The first is the males of seemingly all species compete with one another in various choreographed or non-choreographed behaviors designed to win the attention of a female or females.

The second important factor is the female or females of seemingly all species who, upon observing these behaviors and keying in on desired traits and/or characteristics, chooses which male, or males, she will allow to mate with her.

Of course mating and courting rituals vary from one species to the next; however, no matter their performers and/or platforms they all have at their core the very same and deliberate purpose. That same and deliberate purpose exists so males may offer a female, or females, an opportunity to judge their potential as perhaps protectors/ providers, and producers of strong offspring; although the two former potentialities is likely not the case in all instances the latter in all probability is.

If one reflects upon the very real probability that the

animal kingdom of today with regard to the behaviors of its creatures' mating and/or courting rituals is likely not evolved at all from what it once was then one cannot help but to come upon some very intriguing questions; such as: If animals today are behaving the same way they always have then would it not stand to reason that the human animal of that time behaved in the same way for the same reasons? What does this observation tell us about the dynamics of the true and natural order of Life? What is that true and natural order? With regard to the human animal is this order still in place? If not...then what happened?

To this very day the human animal is the same animal it has always been. Since the earliest beginnings of its collective evolutionary progression nature has imprinted it with the most basic yet most powerfully profound driving forces required to continue its existence. The first two of these forces, the need for food and shelter, have quite arguably always directed both Woman and Man in precisely the same ways for precisely the same reasons.

The third in all probability is equally behooving, recreationally speaking, to Woman and Man; but has two very different meanings for each. It is in this particular microcosm of Life that we can begin to see where and why the truest instinctualities of the female human animal and the male human animal begin to diverge. And it is through this window into the human animal's soul wherein we can feel, know and ultimately understand the way of the natural order of things as Life has always intended it.

The significant differences between the instinctual foundations of the female human animal and the male human animal become apparent and remain so when one takes a closer look into the realm of the sexual world. It is within the context of this uncomplicated sphere of existence where the truest essence of each is revealed. Plainly stated it is as follows: The female human animal and the male human animal are simple creatures with simple needs. These needs are and always have been inherently hardwired into each in quite the same manner save for in one very critical way.

The proverbial gravitational pull of the drive to fulfill sexual desires is arguably exerted upon both the female animal and the male human animal in equal proportions. This is to say that not one craves, seeks, or engages in more sexual intercourse than the other and that naturally speaking…the female human animal and the male human animal are exactly the same in these instances. What is different is the *WHY* of it all.

To this point in our evolutionary progression nature has never allowed the male human animal to carry, birth, or nurture Life from within him. Therefore he has remained disconnected from the truest quintessence of the act of sexual intercourse in all ways except for in a highly superficial manner. His is a driving force grounded deeply in nothing more than self-gratification.

From the depths of man's instinctual core there comes an

unrelenting hunger for sexual intercourse. The mere thought of it conjures feelings of much anticipated sensory satisfaction. He hungers for it because it is supremely pleasurable; nothing more…nothing less. Since the male human animal's beginning, whether it was upon the vast plains or in the cavernous dwellings of the world, he has been instinctually driven toward seeking and finding a mate so that he might be able to repeatedly engage in sexual intercourse for the purposes of perpetuating self-gratification.

The male human animal is simple. He has three essential, primitive needs/ wants/ desires. He needs/ wants/ desires for food. He needs/ wants/ desires for shelter. He needs/ wants/ desires for sex. Of these three deeply ingrained instinctual behaviors, sex will always be his primary focus. If he must choose between them he would rather be wet and go hungry than be without the intimate feel of a mate. The male human animal inherently knows this to be true and when he is pressed to deny or accept this he will undoubtedly agree he is as has just been said. This observation is plain. It is fair and it is just. This particular instinctual knowledge is one half of the equation that comprises the natural order of things with regard to the human animal.

The female human animal is a different story... for a different reason. Bear in mind none of the aforementioned with regard to the male human animal is meant to suggest in any, way, shape or form the female human animal does not, or cannot extract, the same measures of pleasure from sexual intercourse as her male counterpart. For her the rewards of the immediacy of the act itself are likely the same, if not more intense, as they are for him. However, the source of her proverbial gravitational pull toward the need to fulfill the desire for sexual intercourse originates not from an egocentric instinctuality, but rather an altruistic one.

Through a holistic reasoning entirely unknown to us Nature selected one half of the majority of all life-forms on this planet to be the vessel by which their offspring could be conceived, nurtured, and birthed so they might continue to exist long after they have left the physical planes of this world. Nature did not make Woman. Nature did not make Man. Nature simply gave rise to life. It was the male human animal who named us so and it was he who dissolved our marriage to Nature itself. In doing so he initiated the unraveling of Life's simple formula for existence.

Woman, as the male human animal so named her, was chosen by Nature to bear the weight of the most significant processes of pro-creation. She was gifted with the physiology & instincts necessary to do so. One half of the seed of life lives within her. It is watered with the other half living within him. Within her the halves become one and within her the one seed is nurtured and life begins anew.

The female human animal, like the male human animal, is beautiful in the simplicity of her needs/ want/ desires. From the depths of her instinctual core, however, she is not solely driven by the superficialities of the pleasures of sexual intercourse. She is motivated by something greater than her mate or herself. Nature has seen to this. The female human animal is powerful because she is the one ultimately endowed by Nature to ensure our immortality.

It is she who carries, births, and nurtures our children from within her body. It is she who has had bestowed upon her the indispensable instincts necessary to seeking out and finding in her mate the qualities most suited to providing a more than viable opportunity for their offspring to live long and prosper (thank you, Mr. Spock). For this reason she is completely and absolutely connected to the truest essence of the act of sexual intercourse in certainly more than just a superficial manner.

The female human animal knows this to be inherently true… even to this very day. When she is pressed about the accuracy of this observation she will confirm it is so. And this particular instinctual knowledge is the other, more profound, half of the equation that comprises the natural order of things with regard to the human animal. As with the male human animal…this observation is plain. It is simple. It is fair. It is just.

The way of the natural order of things has always been clearly defined. The male human animal lives to survive. He is inherently driven to keep himself in a state of equilibrium. He needs/ wants/ desires to eat. He needs/ wants/ desires to be protected from the elements. Most of all he needs/ wants/ desires the sensory satisfaction sexual intercourse grants. He is selfish…inherently so. The female human animal, on the other hand, is inherently driven to find equilibrium for those whom will come from within her. She needs/ wants/ desires to seek and find a mate worthy of immortality. She is self-less…inherently so.

Once upon a time when the human animal was young and the world was already very old the female human animal and the male human animal knew, understood, and respected the natural order of things. The female human animal held firm to the throne of the world. The male human animal held firm to his place as her second. Life's simple formula was in perfect harmony with the soul of the world. But this did not remain so.

Gradually Man's egocentric sense of self evolved into something dark and its result was the severing of the natural order of things. Through the darkness of his self inflicted isolation he wandered; blind to everything, save for one thing. It was there Man found his "reason" for going against Life and ultimately bringing about its betrayal. It was in this darkness he found and embraced resentment. For he knew and felt the inherent power of the female human animal and he knew it would always be hers. He knew he was nothing more than just Man; a mere survivor and seeker of self-indulgence. He wanted what she had. He commenced on his path of deceit, manipulation, and coercion. He would steal what was naturally and righteously hers. And so began the greatest tragedy of all.

-On When It All Began-

Once upon a long time ago the human animal lived in small, nomadic clans. Anthropological and archeological records indicate these clans likely subsisted on the offerings of the land and the quarry hunted. These days of hunting and gathering were how the human animals of that past appear to have ensured their clans' survival; that is of course until the advent of agriculture when a new evolution began.

It was with the dawn of this new innovation, approximately 10,000 to 12,000 years ago, that the human animal found a way to literally cultivate a new world order; one which effectively made moot the need to constantly follow its resources. This made it possible for the human animal to plant its proverbial roots.

The human animal evolved into something a little bit more than what it had been and because this was now the case existing and flourishing within a society capable of cultivating its own food resources was now not just possible, but probable. The uncertainty of living a nomadic life was largely over. No more was survival strictly contingent upon chance or the human animal's skills and blind luck as hunter and gatherer. The invariable competition for resources between nomadic human animals was no longer absolute.

Things were likely off to a good start. But, as is generally the case when groups of any individuals converge to live as one in a relatively short amount of time, there probably arose some societal growing pains. This societal evolution created its own gravity. In doing so it began pulling more and more human animals into its center.

It must have occurred to some of the actors within this new society that although the procuring of food may have ceased to be the hardship it once was there were now other worries to consider.

The inhabitants of these new societies continued to feel the same sting of their individual needs/ wants/ and desires. Each still needed to eat, each still needed to be sheltered, and each still desired to ensure the continuation of the species. But…what to do?

Under these particular circumstances it is easy to appreciate how the new promise of increased survivability offered by agriculture was enough to initiate the cultural change that resulted. It was as if an evolutionary explosion of accelerated logic took hold and expanded the human animal's capabilities of comprehending its own abilities.

Bearing this in mind it is logical to conclude what must have become quite apparent to the human animals inhabiting these new societies not long after the birth of their newfound dynamic; not all possessed the understanding, talent, or perhaps dedication necessary to become the skilled farmers needed to make certain the productivity of whatever land they lived upon.

This coupled with a collective and concrete realization there were still other crucial societal needs to be met caused a further phenomenon; a division of labor. If some could not or would not become productive stewards of the land then they could and would contribute to the society in other productive and absolutely necessary ways. And those ways were ones for which each of those individuals had an affinity and/ or talent.

As Socrates explains in Plato's *Republic*: "A State . . . arises . . . out of the needs of mankind; no one is self-sufficing, but all of us have many wants. . . As we have many wants, and many persons are needed to supply them, one takes a helper for one purpose and another for another; and when these partners and helpers are gathered together in one habitation the body of inhabitants is termed a State. . . . And they exchange with one another, and one gives, and another receives, under the idea that the exchange will be for their good."

This articulation of the eventual evolution of a society sets forth the idea that larger and larger groups of people living together will come to a point in their societal development wherein they recognize it is collectively more behooving to have those who are good at performing very specific tasks perform and complete only those tasks for which they have an affinity or special training (Specialization). This type of structured productivity serves to ensure all the needs of the members of that society are met; rather than expecting each individual to complete all tasks in hopes of providing for all of their own individual needs.

Every individual taking on every task in order to ensure all of their individual needs are achieved amounts to perhaps all of those tasks getting completed, but ironically none of those tasks getting completed well. This ultimately would result in a loss of labor/ production. This type of unstructured individual effort would likely be of minimal benefit to the majority of individuals and in no way would greatly serve to positively impact the society in which those individuals live. It would be the law of diminishing returns… galore.

Once the male human animal recognized the significance of what Plato coined Specialization he implemented it, i.e., the farmer farmed, the cobbler cobbled, the carpenter constructed, & the blacksmith manipulated metal. In doing this the male human animal came upon another even greater realization. The throne of the world was primed for a coup d'état and the female human animal's throne was now in the sights of the male human animal's greed. The male human animal saw and seized his opportunity to take this division of labor a step further and perhaps he used its legitimacy to devise a specific sub-category of specialization developed specially for the female human animal. Perhaps it could have been called something akin to Domestics 101.

It was at this point that the male human animal made his bold and deliberate move and set into motion the world's greatest atrocity. Amongst his fellow males he conspired to deny our female human animal virtually all access to newfound knowledge and skill; academic, industrial, and otherwise in the hope she might finally realize and accept her true place under his thumb. Her place would no longer be atop the throne of the world, but rather within confining walls. Domesticity became the Specialization for which she would be groomed.

As man refined his skills and knowledge in this *brave* and bold new world he began to understand there was more than just a pragmatic value to what he was producing. He began to understand he could exchange the goods he created with others for that which he could not, or would not, produce himself. He began to understand that trade was, in and of itself, a perfect institution to provide for the needs of the societal collective and it could achieve this goal in a consistent and high-quantity manner. As life proceeded within this new agrarian and quasi-industrious society man became more and more gluttonous. His female human animal counterpart, on the other hand, became more and more accepting of the domesticity forced upon her.

The male human animal continued to perform his specialized tasks and refine his specialized goods-producing skills. He continued to exchange these goods with others on grander and grander scales. In doing so, he eventually opened the door to yet another new awareness; the idea that some goods were endowed with more worth than others due to their increased demand, specificity of usability, and perhaps their diverse usefulness.

In any society there are commodities which are perceived more valuable than others. It would appear this has always been so. In this beginning it was agriculture which helped to concretely establish this principle in a whole new light. Perhaps this became so simply because some vegetables were found to be more desirable than others or one tool was seen as more diverse and useful than another.

Preferred commodities acquired higher exchange rates because of their perceived increased value. This is to say a producer/ owner of the most highly valued stuff could obtain more of other lesser valued stuff in direct exchange for the more desirable stuff that producer/ owner possessed.

Pointing out the birth of that particular concept in that new and ever-expanding society is essential in perhaps showing where the male human animal found what he had been looking for since tricking, manipulating, and coercing the female human animal into her domestic cage. In that time and in that moment he found a way to complete her domestication and ultimately crush her spirit; that she might never remember her truest essence and never rise to challenge him in any capacity.

Remember... the male human animal initiated and facilitated this discourse by denying new knowledge and new skill to his female human animal counterpart. Controlling knowledge meant he controlled all the leverage in this new societal existence. Leverage meant he could now dictate and shape behavior.

The shaping and dictating of behavior had been the whole of the female human animal's divine ability as granted by nature. It was she who was entrusted to carry, birth, & nurture life from within her own body. It was she whom the male human animal followed. It was she from whom he took his cues. And it was she who allowed him to be a part of her. She did not force this upon him. There was no need; for of his place he was always aware. But this appears to have been what the male human animal plotted so methodically to utterly destroy through his *brave* and bold new agrarian world.

Unto himself in greater and greater quantities he began to gather the most valuable and sought-after commodities in this new way of life. In doing so the male human animal set the stage for the complete de-evolution of the natural dynamic between him and the female human animal.

Possessing more and more desirable stuff seems to have meant accumulating more and more power; albeit perceived, but perhaps perceived hard enough by the rest of the male human animals so as to render this power *real* within this infant society.

It was here… in this microcosm of big-bang-think that the male human animal de-constructed the one humanimal into two separate entities. It was here he spewed forth his segregate idea of Man & Woman. It was here he tricked, manipulated, and coerced the female human animal into thinking, feeling, and then believing that she no longer needed rely on the instinctual knowledge granted to her by nature.

Embracing agriculture meant leaving behind the nomadic lives of hunters and gatherers. The human animal gained a greater control over its own destiny and therefore began to thrive like never before. Primitive though it may have been the female human animal and male human animal began to live as actors in a society structured much differently than ever before.

Cultivated and nurtured in such a way as to *help* the female human animal believe she was doing her part the male human animal became at slowly and surely stealing the world. He initiated and instituted a new world order; one that did not follow the natural order of things. It was one he must absolutely rule and control at every expense; for he was selfish and craved what had always been hers... power inherent.

He knew she must be conditioned into something other than herself. This had to be done for once-upon-a-time when the human animal lived with the land as opposed to just on it the natural order of things was as it was always meant to be. Life's simple, yet effective, formula and The Three Truths were in place and the world was good; but its fate seems to have been sealed when the male human animal recognized that within the *progression* of this new society these essential ingredients of success could be challenged. The male human animal recognized it was possible to subvert nature, but what to do?

It was a tricky proposition to be sure. The small clans in which the human animal had existed prior to this agricultural evolution may likely have been matriarchal in nature; there appears to be nothing in the fossil record that may indicate otherwise. It was the female human animal who decided who to choose as mate, it was she whom he would seek to impress ritually; begging her approval. And it was she who was granted the inherent tools necessary to ensure the survival of the species. It was she who was the center of it all and he was still merely a survivor and seeker of self-indulgence. The male human animal inherently understood, respected, and accepted the natural order of things and thus was his part in keeping nature's simple, yet effective, plan for life balanced.

The advent of agriculture seems to have changed more

than just the need for the human animal to constantly follow its resources for survival. Agriculture appears to have changed how the human animal perceived prosperity. Success in this new society with its newfound knowledge and newfound industrial skills did not appear to merely mean the end of uncertainty with regard to being fed, clothed, and sheltered. The more significant thing that appeared to have been altered was the reality that no longer was it enough to have and use only what was absolutely necessary.

Excess appears to have become the norm as did the realization that others would likely go without the basic necessities. This particular time and this particular place, perhaps, was the birthplace of the apathy we all continue to know to this day. The conceptualization and embracing of material wealth became the latest standard of existence and surviving in this new world order meant the male human animal must commit to *teaching* the female human animal she no longer had to trust her instincts or her soul when choosing a mate. No longer should she seek the primitively pure character, emotional, and physical qualities her instincts and her soul pulled her towards.

The male human animal convinced her she must forsake Nature because he had what she now needed and that was material wealth; it was here the slow murder of integrity of the natural order of things began. The superior and natural qualities of the male human animal's inherent traits and qualities of instinctual character no longer were necessary considerations to be held in high regard when it came to the choosing of a mate... at least this is what he wanted her to believe. What mattered most now was only how much more stuff one male human animal had than another.

He unleashed an unrelenting attack upon her senses. He used his wealth to *teach* her that she needed the material items he possessed in order to survive ...to exist ... to increase viability of her offspring. In short... an abundance of material wealth predestined a higher quality of life. This was essentially the same formula Life had given the human animal to begin with, but this version…his version… was twisted, turned upside down, and perverted to meet the male human animal's needs/ wants/ desires on his terms alone. The inherent qualities that originally made him stand out amongst other male human animals were now dismissed as unnecessary. These very special qualities within him were now replaced by very mundane quantities of stuff outside of him.

The attack was strategic and subtle in its ferocity. It had to be… for she was no fool after all and subtlety was required in order to get her to complete the betrayal of her Self. First she was relegated to the domesticities of home life with claims by him that this was where her truest power lay. Next she was methodically denied new knowledge and new skill. Last was his overwhelming and overstated proclamation that the most wealth defined the most superior mate. With this onslaught of cancerous mantras the male human animal commenced to achieving his goal; stripping our female human animal of her truest essence and turning her into just one more possession. Never has violence so obscene been so gentle and unassuming in its utter destruction.

-On What Happened Next-

It was impressive. In what seems like the blink of an eye our female human animal was deposed from her throne as the absolute ruler of this world; the one Nature always intended to be hers. She was ushered to the back seat of every proverbial bus yet to pass throughout our history.

First into her psyche it was pounded and then into her soul it was ground that she was no longer necessary as she once was. At the hands of the male human animal, who now called himself Man, she became woman; a significantly lesser version of her ridiculously single-minded male counterpart. Man allowed her to believe she was still the queen, but now instead of safe guarding our survival and maintaining Life's simple plan her existence was devolved into that of a mere servant for impostor kings. Her most significant contribution to the state of the world strayed from the safeguarding of the natural order of things to the mere keeping of a clean home. She was now a prisoner of Man and his twisted ideals.

Impostor kings rule impostor kingdoms and Man's world has been a falsehood since he conceived it; gauge the extent to which he has expended his efforts in order to build and maintain it. Along the way he has sought to relentlessly blame our female human animal for what he says she has done. As time passed this violence perpetrated upon her evolved from subtle, in-direct actions at its infancy, to blatant and spiteful words intended to finish convincing her that she was never worthy of her place as the true ruler of this world. Man told woman the natural order of things was a lie and she had been its fortunate and most gratuitous beneficiary.

Man was no fool. He understood that although subtlety may have been enough to initiate the re-structuring of the natural order of things he required additional tools to guarantee her slavery that his male progeny might continue to hold sway over her for all time. Oral traditions and the spoken word can carry a society only so far. There is a tendency for substantial information to get lost in translation. However, when an idea is set in writing there is the effect of casting that idea, no matter what it may be, in proverbial stone.

The written word is powerful. To this there can be no refutation. Who is to say when, where, or how it specifically began? Who is to a male human animal was responsible for its birth? Who is to say a female human animal did not? No matter its origins there is one thing that is empirically certain; the written word serves one significant purpose. It always has and it always will.

The written word is history... our history. To say it is an absolutely true historical account of our times past would not be entirely accurate; for as has been known throughout the ages of our inscribed world...History is written by the victors!

The written word is a record that something has occurred.

It is a record of *how* that something occurred. It is a record of how to ensure that that something can happen again and it is a record to ensure, perhaps, that an unwanted something is not repeated.

Man used the written word capably. He used it to pass on the new knowledge and the new skills he had acquired. He used it to instruct the men after him just how to maintain an iron grip on the world. And in his most devious fashion Man used the written word to perpetuate the oppression of she who he now called woman.

In the hands of Man it was the written word that guaranteed the steady de-evolution of the natural order of things just as he envisioned it. In the hands of Man it was the written word that ultimately solidified the explicit roles women and men were to play in the new world order he created. How else to make certain all knew, "understood", and accepted their place within the new world order?

As with all other innovative technology and skill

discovered in and around this once-upon-a-time the practices necessary to learn and master the written word were withheld from our female human animal. She was purposefully denied access to that which could have led to the liberation of her mind and of her soul from the enslaving grip of her selfish and greedy male human animal counterpart.

History, as it is written, has shown the aforementioned observation to appear more true than not. As such it can be logically surmised that perhaps throughout our history the bulk of texts used to indoctrinate society with rules founded and grounded in the exultation of Man may very likely have been authored by men. One must ask… What female human animal would promote such violence upon herself? Could it be this is why many texts appear to share common threads with regards to what is generally expected and accepted behavior when it comes to women? Perhaps this is also why men, to this day, continue to rule the world despite their seemingly best efforts to utterly destroy all vestiges of hope.

Scrutinize this closely and a single question is born: How can it be varying texts originating in various expanses across time appear to espouse similar beliefs and/ or expectations of women? The answer is simple. This phenomenon is likely directly linked to the inherent feelings of powerlessness the male human animal has carried within him since our beginnings. From the onset the male human animal has known , deep within his core, that he was deemed by Nature to be nothing more than one half of a means to an end; immortality. The male human animal has always known his place. He knows it to this day. He understands he is a significant and necessary piece of the process that is our immortality, but he also knows in the grand scheme of things he is expendable after his one significant and necessary duty is fulfilled.

No man likes knowing he is necessary only to a point. No man will accept he can never be as important as his female human animal counterpart. No man wants to accept he is helpless to alter this reality. Every man would have every female human animal believe quite the opposite: He **is** necessary absolutely, he **is** as important (if not more so) than she, & he **can** force evolution upon the natural order of things. Man **is** as he says. He has written it so.

When and where in time did this written word come into being? It can be postulated until the end of days as to who first conceived, sculpted, & employed the written word. All that can be said for certain is, whenever or wherever this happened, the door into the human animal's collective intellectual potential was opened further than it had ever been before.

Communication between human animals became more than the mere exchanging of rudimentary expressions and/ or gestures meant to convey messages, instructions, expectations, or warnings. No longer was the fulfillment of a reality mostly contingent upon sheer happenstance. In point of fact a specific reality could now be achieved in a very specific way and the process could be repeated to continually achieve the same specific results. Luck, for the most part, was cast out of the proverbial pre-History window. It was a paradigm shift that eventually planted the seeds of the male human animal's coup d'état against his female human animal counterpart. And in our world...our "civilized" world... the overthrow has been more religiously grounded than not. Breathe.

Admittedly, I do not profess to be any expert on any religion of the world; nor do I assert to any degree that I am widely read or familiar with any religious text, custom, or tradition. I operate merely from a point of complete empirical observation. This is the purest reality of the origins of what I am trying to convey to you. I fully understand what the reckoning of this confession can likely mean for my credibility. Even so... undeterred I shall remain for what is to be said MUST be said; for your sake... for my sake... for the world's.

And so a crossroads we have reached. It is in this moment… in this space…in this time… that you are hereby challenged to decide what you shall do next. Will you keep ingesting my words and my thoughts? Or will you allow perhaps deeply ingrained, strongly held personal beliefs and/ or prejudices to dismiss that which you have come across to this point?

To press on is not to sanctify the betrayal of your Self or of your soul. Perhaps what you are simply choosing to do is view life from a different angle. What is offered ultimately is an opportunity. It is an opportunity to see that which you likely have been blinded to throughout your time on this blue and green planet.

Consider what you may gain against that which you may be compelled to question; strong, long held, & deeply ingrained beliefs. Consider that you are more than what you and our society have allowed you to be. Consider it is your absolute right as a beautiful and primitive human animal to remain more connected, than you have ever been, to every living thing and every living being in this world of ours.

You are where it must start; for you were there at the very dawn of our existence and it is you who must bring us back to our beginning that this world may live simply once again.

-On The *Word* of God-

First and foremost it is necessary to acknowledge the existence of God has neither been proven nor dis-proven at any point in our history. Simply put God **IS** for some and God **IS NOT** for others. Whatever the case (your case) may be there is something that remains empirically certain. It cannot be denied that God, in some form or another and by whatever name, has had the greatest amount of influence upon the evolution of most of the world's largest and "civilized" societies.

Depending on where in the world you may have been born, lived, or simply visited it is almost certain that God is, or has been, there. What is not certain is what shape or form God is, or has been, present. God has many, many faces; of this you are aware. And although the face of God melts and morphs with the different lands and the different peoples of the world, the message of God remains essentially the same; be good to each other… take care of each other. But this is not the way of God as it is written by man and as it is sheathed in this largely religious world.

God is not religion and religion is not God. To say that God and religion are synonymous is to insist that God literally penned written instructions on what the expectations of the human animal must be forever more. How much longer will we allow ourselves to endure this fallacy? God wrote nothing; save for that which had already been etched onto your very heart long before you were even born unto this world.

What is written by God swims in your soul and in your blood; the Three Truths. The Three Truths tell us: It is better to co-exist and cooperate than not. Fight only when absolutely necessary. Kill only when truly defending your life or the lives of those whom you have been entrusted to protect. God wrote nothing more and God wrote nothing less.

There are many who will employ the circular argument

that I cannot possibly know anything of God because I am not a person of religion. To them I have torpedoed any credibility I might have championed with my confession that I am no expert on any religions and am largely ignorant of their finer details. "What does he know?" They may ask or perhaps more to the point…shout! Perhaps they will demand to have me burned at the stake! Nonetheless, it is a good question. What **do** I know after all?

I am master of nothing you, in your heart, do not already command. I hold what you hold. I know what you know; belief. It is the belief that in your soul swims the answer to the riddle of what is good and what is bad. This is the very essence of what God etched onto your heart since our ancestors began. And it is exhibited in our very instincts that absolutely are The Three Truths: It is better to cooperate and co-exist than not, fight only when absolutely necessary, & kill only when truly defending your life or the lives of those whom you have been entrusted to protect. The Three Truths are self-evident for we did not have to learn them in a classroom nor from any book.

They have been within us since before our day one. There is no erasing them; no matter how hard one may try. They shall remain in our blood and in our collective soul ever more; a gifted inheritance bequeathed upon us by our beautiful, beautiful and absolutely primitive ancestors. And we shall bequeath them upon all whom shall come after us. For **this** is the will of **God**! This observation is plain. It is simple. It is fair and it is just.

Stop. Listen to your soul. Hear the voice of God… within you. You will recognize this to be true. But sure as The Three Truths live and breathe, they live and breathe in obscurity in the world of today. For as much as they can never be erased from within us they, like all the rest of our finer individual qualities, can be ignored and allowed to grow stale.

What happened? How did it come to pass The Three

Truths were, and are, fundamentally forgotten... forsaken to the world at large? The answer is simple. Man deliberately wrote them out of the equation of our existence. He did this so well that over time...long periods of time... he ingrained us with the bold belief that The Three Truths do not exist and never have.

From very early on man taught us that instincts were primal, savage, untamed things not meant to be relied upon by beings blessed with such supernatural *intelligence* and *reasoning* as ours. It is a scandal long in the making and even longer in its lifespan; for its life began when man first saw his chance to steal the stewardship of the world from his female human animal counterpart all those eons ago.

Man knew, however, his impure efforts would all be for naught unless he could find some way to ensure his grand conspiracy's legacy. To this end he made a weapon of the written word. For he realized it was a force as destructive as it was creative. Here before him lay the means to accomplish his ultimate goal; the theft of the world. It would have been so very easy, but for one minor problem; the details.

Details are funny things; leave them out and questions abound. Whittle them down to finer and finer points and questions and doubts grow smaller and smaller until all that may be left is blind belief. I will call that faith. And faith, like everything central to our existence, can be shaped, molded, and pounded into something other than what it was meant to be.

Long ago man realized the power of spoken language and its ability to influence… to inspire… to mobilize the masses. When the written word arrived he quickly recognized it not only possessed similar qualities, but it could be more powerful than its spoken-word cousin; for it, unlike that oral cousin, could be literally set in stone. So it became that man charged the written word with assisting him to steal the world.

But, what to write …exactly? What plausible

explanation could man offer his inherently more powerful female human animal counterpart for what he was to attempt? How could she be convinced to sanction his filth? Surely she would never simply just hand him the throne of the world for the sake of satiating his greed and lust for power. The answer to his conundrum became clear; religion. In the end it was simple as simple math; religion + man's god = M3(Mass Mind Manipulation). It was brilliant.

Religion as defined by Merriam-Webster is: 1 *a*: the state of a religious <a nun in her 20th year of *religion*> *b (1)*: the service and worship of God or the supernatural

(2): commitment or devotion to religious faith or observance 2: a personal set or institutionalized system of religious attitudes, beliefs, and practices 3 *archaic*: scrupulous conformity:

CONSCIENTIOUSNESS 4: a cause, principle, or system of beliefs held to with ardor and faith.

What this definition does not tell you is that religion is a manufacture born of man; born of man…ironic. Religion, not life, was intelligently designed and crafted in a very specific context for a very specific reason. Much, much care was taken to ensure the proper nurturing and attention were paid it at just the right intervals so as to bring about the cementing of Religion as the end all be all of the human animal's entire existence upon our blue and green planet. Funny; I write these thoughts…and I am reminded of a once-upon-a-time of my own.

I do not recall his name, but long ago we worked in the same place. One night we were talking… about Religion. He showed me something he had written and told me I should read it. I took the hefty work home and for a few days I tried, but as I am sure his words were meant for me… they were not FOR me; they scorned, bastardized, and chastised me for my very being… for I did not think, feel, or believe as he did.

His words put me down so I put them down and never picked them up again. I do not remember what happened to what I am sure was that young man's very well-intentioned work after I returned it to him. What I do remember, however, was the title. I remember thinking it was more profound than he probably understood, but not in the way he might have thought. That young man's work was called:

> **B**asic
> **I**nstructions
> **B**efore
> **L**eaving
> **E**arth

I was left wondering… If the instructions are so basic then why does the work contain so many, many pages? Alas, perhaps it was because he may have considered his work a religious text in its own right.

Again…God and Religion are not one in the same. God is inherent; Religion is not. God swims in everyone and in everything; Religion does not. God is in your blood and God is in your soul; no matter your insistence that God is not and no matter your personal beliefs, opinions, or politics. Religion is capable of no such feat.

Once-upon-a-time we knew and we believed all of the

above, but along the way we were slowly led to think, feel, and then believe exactly the opposite. Man manufactured Religion for this sole/ soul (take your pick) purpose. By force and by fear of threat we were fed Religion, its tenets, and its insistence that God was it and it was God. So said the powers-that-be.... so screamed the vengeful, terrible, and frightened masses!

But it was a hoodwink; for Religion was, and is, a creation born solely of man's warped will to dominate others; chiefly his inherently more powerful female human animal counterpart. As hammer and chisel did man use the written word to carve over time, in meticulous detail, this thing called Religion; that it might mimic the face of God just enough to make permanent its twisted goals whilst hiding its truest face.

Man built Religion on the sheer premise that there lay the stone-hammer by which to drive the final binding nail thru the female human animal's heart which would all but complete her crucifixion or the crushing of her warrior-spirit by the carefully aimed rock used to stone her. How else to explain stories and orations *authored* by God denouncing the virtues and intentions of the female human animal? How else to question her worthiness, yet designate her worth as property? How else to justify violence against her? How else to espouse the belief that man was endowed by God to have dominion over all? How else to infect the world en masse with madness and propagate it as philosophy wrought in golden *wisdom*?

Marry this with the fact that man, throughout earliest written histories, conscientiously strived to deny the female human animal the key by which to unlock the power of the written word and you will see what I see. You will feel what I feel. You will know what I, in my deepest core, know. Anger will begin to rise within you.

Before you a picture of man deafening, silencing, blinding, and binding the female human animal will emerge;

hear no *Evil*, see no *Evil*, speak no *Evil*, do no *Evil*. Sound familiar? Could it be the *Evil* spoken of here refers to the female human animal? For in translations and interpretations of old and new, as professed by man, she is responsible for tragedy upon tragedy befalling the world of man.

Perhaps the conversation went something like this once-upon-a-long-time-ago:

Man #1: (concerned & guilt-ridden; for there were at least a few) –*What we have done, and what we are doing, is not good. We have spat on ourselves. We have severed our better half from our own whole being. We have created that which was never meant to exist; an imbalance in life. We must do this no longer. We must teach her to read. We must teach her to write. We must remember that we are not life; only a mere piece of the soul of the world and therefore not granted any authority under God to force that which was never meant to be compulsory.*

Man #2: (greedy & lusting for power) - *Are you mad?*
Listen to yourself! You... are a fool. Our life is riches. Our
life is power. Our life is pleasure-filled. Our life and how we
came to it is none of her concern! Let her hear of the
atrocities we have committed and she may roar in truest
revolt! Let her see what we have done and she will be moved
to action! She will remember from whence she came and
strip us of our false kingdoms! We must not allow her to
know! She must know only that which we have deemed
worthy of her lowly state!

Man #1: (concerned & guilt-ridden) - *It is a fallacy for*
we are not the vessels of God. She is what we shall never be;
for we are but a drop of life to her ocean of salvation and
immortality! It is not for us to decide who shall hold sway
over this world. We are her lesser and we, to a man, know
this in our deepest souls. We must reverse this course before
it is believed as the natural order of things. We must do this
for the sake of our daughters... and for our daughters'

daughters. We must do this for the sake of the world.

Man #3: (also greedy & lusting for power) - *This will not do! Too hard we have worked to ensure that that which we have stolen remains ours! Much toil has been exerted to trick, manipulate, coerce, & deceive our way onto a most favorable position to inherit the throne of the world. Do you propose we tell her?! To this she would not take kindly. And should she know we would all be left to rely upon our character, our mettle, and our purest being to win a mate. I am a man of worth in wealth not a man wealthy in worth of character. I suspect the rest of you are much the same as I. If we teach her to remember who she was we seal our fates. She will know wealth does not equate worthiness and she will not grant us immortality. Why should this be? Especially since our god and our religion have given us power and wealth enough to buy her. Nay, keep her deaf. Keep her blind. Keep her silent. Keep her binded; for she believes the lie and we are reaping every last reward* *because of it.*

Man #1: (concerned & guilt-ridden) – *But it is a crime against nature... against God! The soul of the world yearns for equilibrium; without it we but wander through our lives as nothing more than mere survivors. Will you reduce us to scavengers whose offense against God will ultimately be revealed? For that is how tales such as these always have ended. In the end we will be despised and we will be reviled for what we have done. I tell you...this is not necessary. This is wrong. This is not the will of God!*

Man #3: *The will of God? And what knowledge of the will of God can thou possibly proclaim to possess? Nothing says I! WE are the masters of all that is written and all that is read; WE are the will of God! WE are the masters of knowledge and skill; industrial, intellectual, philosophical, and otherwise! And WE shall continue to be their greatest champions. WE must be; for not to be is to relinquish that which we have strived so hard to take from her; to fail is to* *accept our place as her second. I am a man! I am second to*

no woman! I, and you and you and you, merit more than the

scraps of elementary existence God reserved for us from the

beginning! The will of God is ours to write and it is ours to

record as we see fit. It is ours to shape in whatever manner

suits us best; for whom else exemplifies the will to do what is

necessary in order to steal the world, but WE?!

Man #2 (Also zealously preaching to Man# 1): *Yes,*

Yes! It is all so simple! Why is this difficult for you to see and

seemingly more difficult for you to embrace? It will not be

without difficulties and perhaps it take will much time, but it

is all so very simple; simple as sin and She will never have to

know. Imagine… one bloodless coup and the world will be

ours for all time. Our god's words and our god's wisdom

shall be our gentle hammer and tender spike. No

bludgeoning required; for that would only alert her to the

extraordinary. Subtlety and sweetness shall be our allies. To

approach this any differently would be to risk exposing our truest hearts and minds. Do not be a fool brother! Come with us and reap what we shall sow! Perhaps not all men shall be granted riches and wealth, but most certainly all men shall be granted dominion over her!

Man #1 (Unconvinced; speaking to both): *It is not I who is the fool for I see and feel unerringly what you do not. I see the dark clouds of treachery and feel the thunder of betrayal fast encroaching upon our sisters; set to let loose a black rain of sorrow that will take the form of the chains of her enslavement! I see bitterness before me personified and taste its vengeful arrogance! I feel hateful hearts hell-bent on satiating the imagined pain of imagined slights! I see before me that which is void of honor, loyalty, and integrity! I see unworthiness to God and I shall call you both brothers no more! Nay! I shall not permit your madness to live!*

Man #2 (cackling smugly): *No one is asking your permission... brother (caked in sarcasm). You are but being informed of what is to come as a mere courtesy. Be grateful* *you have received as much; for you in truth, I now see, are just as weak and feeble as She! In point of fact I am no longer certain you ever have been a man! Go on! Tell whom you will tell! Tell them what you have heard here! Who will listen?! No one! For what approaches is too masterful to be halted and it is too absurd to justify even a modicum of credulity! And that is why it will succeed! So... go forth and spread your good word that the devil has arrived and is walking among the living. No one will believe you... brother (drenched now in disdain and disgust). Everyone will believe **YOU** are the one who is mad.*

Man #3 (riding the other's coat-tails): *You and those of your mindthink will suffer... alongside her! She will learn her place! She will learn her unworthiness! By the end of this new and prosperous man-made beginning She will accept them and She will embrace them; dare I say She may even learn to love them as She will come to embrace them as elemental pieces of her very soul. Like stone ground to dust* *we will leave her with no recollection of whom or what She was once-upon-at-time. We will make her our property. We will make her our slave. She will beg for a man to provide… for her… for her children; in her mind all that will matter is a man of wealth no matter his character. For that man will be my son and his son after him and we, from this day hence, will be the servants of our one real god Gold and we will lay claim and waste to whatever we will; including her soul! And you… and your undiscovered righteous brethren will be regulated to obscurity. Sure as I speak it is not lost upon me that you will most certainly not be the only one of your kind; for every war has its would-be heroes. But heed my warning… those who stand against the tempest will feel the wrath of **our** god's words and **our** Religion's tenets! You and your foolish followers will all be painted as frail of mind and of body and of spirit. We will use our god's words to castrate you all. The stage of your extinction will be set; for in the new world order that is coming there will be no room* *for the inconsequential sentimental yearnings of days gone by! Good riddance says I! If you will not follow then your seed shall find no field to sow and immortality will never find you. Our god will kill your moral... your ideological high ground and **it** will gladly murder the potency of her self-worth in slow, slow fashion and She, brother, will be forced to think, feel, and believe that her truest and most singular validating purpose on **our** god's earth will be to be chosen and not to choose. So let it be written... So shall it be done!*

-On History-

One religion led to another and then another until, at last, there eventually came to be two that emerged as more dominant than the rest. I will take it for granted you know to which three I refer. Now … I am not asserting there are only three religions deserving of mention, for in my view they have all played a critical role in what I am professing. What I mean to say is these **B**ig Three **R**eligions, if you will, were all born unto this world from the same root; they are different branches of the same tree and they have dominated and motivated much of man's thinking throughout the course of most of our written history.

Each of the BTRs appears to espouse very powerful and beautiful tenets about how and why their god is the one to follow. Each also appears to make very clear distinctions about the fate of those whom do not follow their particular god and that god's particular teachings. As well each of these BTRs seemingly espouses equally powerful, but detestable, tenets on how man must consider woman. Ironically, each also appears to make subtle, yet undeniable inferences, of the inherent importance of the female human animal. Even more ironic is the empirical fact that said inferences are nothing more than proverbial footnotes to what are the man-dominated chatter/ tenets/ proclamations supposedly held sacred by each of these BTRs.

The only way to justifiably describe what has occurred here is shameful. For the only thing that can be said with any real certainty, with regard to what exactly the BTRs stand for (and all other religions for that matter) is that someone, or some ones, once-upon-a-very-long-time ago had very agreeable ideas and beliefs which resonated most powerfully with many, many people across large swaths of social divisions.

That message remains as simple and as profound today as it was when it was first uttered to the masses: Be good to each other; Take care of each other. Is it any wonder it resonated with so many? Perhaps it was because this message completely and succinctly reinforced that which was already swimming around in our blood; The Three Truths.

Like water spilling over a dam the message spread and spread. Out loud and out spoken did it take hold of more and more human animals; its power inherent in its simplicity. It was not hope the message championed, but more crucially a reality. It was the reality that the human animal was as pure as it had always been and ensuring each other's wellness did not depend upon the love or hate of a benevolent/ malevolent man-made god.

All appeared poised for a return to the natural order of things when the female human animal ruled the world and the male human animal followed her lead; harmony. But something happened along this way and perhaps for the first time ever man's history began to repeat itself.

Slowly and surely man's unrelenting lust of greed and

power showed him that which his forebears recognized; opportunity. Just as those ancestors saw their opportunity to initiate the forced evolution of the natural order of things at the advent of agriculture this subsequent generation of man saw his opportunity to take it all a step further.

He recognized the message's simple yet profound potency and realized it possessed the potential to be used as a vehicle to further establish and protect his creation of a worldwide, male-dominated social dynamic. However this may have all unfolded there is no doubting yet one more empirical fact; almost as quickly as the message appeared on the human animal's landscape were steps taken, by man, to undermine its truest essence.

Prophets, messengers, & espousers alike of this simple yet powerful message (Be good to each other…Take care of each other) were persecuted and dispatched; beaten, broken, burned. Their ultimate demises and the scattering of their followers ensured the message's simplicity would be forgotten to this very day.

History, as it is largely recognized, gives us some very logical and scholarly ideas about how and why this all occurred, but none appear to come remotely close to what may actually have been the truest nature of it all. Perhaps it was not about polytheism vs. monotheism. Nor perhaps might it have been simply about authoritarian rulers fearing the downfall of their empires. No… these may not have been at the real heart of this matter at all. Perhaps this was about continuing the forced amnesia bestowed upon the female human animal all those ages ago. Perhaps this was about man and the continuation of his false kingdoms ruled by his impostor kings.

"But if this is what it was really about…how do you explain the written testimonials of how and why it all happened the way it did? How can you say such things when there are texts (religious and not) that appear to tell us exactly what occurred? Have not people continued to remain in tune with the message's truest essence and is not that why they continue to follow the teachings of specific individuals who supposedly lived so long ago?" These are all very valid and challenging queries. You are right to question.

The response is simple. The breadth of what has been written of our collective humankind history has been written by men; no matter what part of the world you were born or have lived. Men were then as they are now, simple not stupid. When one views this point objectively it is not difficult to grasp the logic behind their specific implementation of the written word. The written word was used to reinforce the *word* of god as conceived and written by man and its primary purpose was to perpetuate the subjugation of the female human animal.

The simple yet powerful message (Be good to each other; Take care of each other) was buried and used as a foundation on which to build man's man-made god-truths. This… this… is how so many today continue to feel the inherent profoundness of that simple message whilst remaining ignorant of what has actually been transpiring. The illusion lives and lives. And since the illusion has been performed on countless stages to countless audiences for so very long in the same specific way it should be no surprise that our reckoning of what is "normal" is what it is. Yet still the message persists. Be good to each other; Take care of each other. It is as if people are not really sure why they keep going back to religion. They just know they should; like a magnet returning to its polar opposite. The point: Simply because something stirs the soul does not mean its essence is necessarily known.

There exists an elementary disconnect between what is felt and why it is felt when it comes to the understanding of what the BTRs, and its cohorts, teach. Insofar as religions go the answer also remains simple; everyone is right and everyone is wrong. Each is on point where they have at their core that same, simple message born so long ago. Be good to each other; Take care of each other.

Where they all consistently appear to go astray is when each inevitably reaches a stance wherein the heretic is told they are a heretic and will suffer the consequences for not believing and behaving as it exclusively prescribes; so stipulate the paths to *true* enlightenment no matter how benignly any particular doctrine may be conveyed.

Be good to each other; Take care of each other. That is all there is. But this message has been historically and incessantly wrapped in layers of man-made lies and those lies have been suffocating the life from The Three Truths ever since. Twist, pervert, repeat… twist, pervert, repeat; such was, and has been, the formula by which man has used the written word to continue his dominance over this world and it has been successful. Twist, pervert, repeat… twist, pervert, repeat… beyond recognition; to the point of utterly destroying all vestiges of hope. As a result the world has been teetering on the edge of oblivion and the female human animal has been a slave under the guise of second class citizenry for all her days of this *civilized* world.

Consider what you know. Consider what you know is nothing more than the obvious. Consider this is not because you have not made attempts to know and feel something more substantial than what has been, and continues to be, offered. Consider you have wanted to see, feel, and know more, but your sight, more precisely your insight, has been blinded or at the very least hindered by the overwhelming obviousness of the world. Consider your thoughts questioning the Hows and Whys of the ordered-ness of this world have not been inconsequential. Consider you have felt the world's lack of equilibrium. Consider that you have been on this journey together with me for some time now and you have yet to disembark. Consider I am no different than you and we possess equal powers of observation. Consider all of these and you may find you have always known what I know. Be good to each other; Take care of each other.

We are all the same. We all want the same thing. We all want harmony. We all want to live in reasonable comfort with no overwhelming sense of fear or foreboding. We all embrace it is better to co-exist and cooperate than not. We all embrace fighting one other is done only when absolutely necessary. We all embrace killing is only truly justified when defending our lives or the lives of those whom we have been entrusted to protect.

Whether we know it or not, or even care to admit, we all embrace The Three Truths. We hold them sacred for although they may be questioned they cannot be denied. I challenge you to delve into your soul and try. The Three Truths are all there... they always have been... but we do not behave like it. There is a hole in our collective soul that is vast and it has been feasting upon and swallowing our human animal-ness since man stole the world from the female human animal and upset the balance of the natural order of things.

Man's history has taught us to think, feel, and believe that we are opposite of what we actually and naturally are; caring, nurturing, and compassionate human animals just being. There is nothing more complex to us than that; for within our simplicity lies our salvation and the salvation of the world. This is a reality man's written history has made more attempts to tear asunder than reinforce; all for the sake of retaining his stranglehold upon the world.

It is not lost on me that my words sound as if I am inferring all of man's written history has been unequivocally wrought with evil intentions. It brings me solace to know the odds of that actually being the case are infinitesimally small. But what a grand conspiracy that would have been! Man's history, as viewed and felt through the eyes and soul of the layperson I know myself to be, is not merely a record of what has transpired in times past, but a beacon of guidance built to light our way into a more translucent future. My...

how oh-so-very cliché that all just sounded! Please accept my sincerest apologies.

No matter how cliché or irreverent the aforementioned may have sounded there is much truth in it. You know this because, like me, a warm and fuzzy feeling bloomed from within the center of your chest and it felt like love when upon those clichéd words you fed. It is has not been the fashion to simply Be good to each other and Take care of each other for a very long time. Today this simple message is viewed with less and less substance and treated more and more as just silly conjecture; for we have all come to play part in a world where indifference rules our hearts rather than compassion and simple, powerful logic.

This is all a symptom of what man's written history has done to us. History has paved the way for the continued acceptance of social mediocrity on larger and larger scales. It has complicated life in ways which were never meant to be and it has convinced the masses the fight to save the soul of the world will always be an uphill and unwinnable battle; not worthy of our most potent energies. But history like life must evolve, or at least it is supposed to; if it does not evolve… if it is not corrected… it will be repeated in all of its impetuous debauchery and we will all ultimately kill our beloved Mother.

It is not that history as it has been written by man must be re-written, but rather more closely scrutinized and reinterpreted. Between the lines of that written history is where we can find our truest story; for all convincing and lasting deceits are built upon hidden truths. The history to which I refer is not the documented grand, adventure in technological, political, or infrastructural advancement upon which all history appears to be grounded. The history to which I refer has everything to do with the societal aspects of our overall growth as a people, or more precisely the lack thereof. Change the angle of view of any perspective and anyone can see there was usually more to an event/

occurrence/ happening than was likely previously thought.

Perhaps all that is required is asking different questions: From where did the concept of marriage emerge and what truly was its originating intention? What did Joan of Arc actually do that warranted her death at the hands of fire? Who was Boudicca and why is she largely absent from the annals of history? Why did Queen Elizabeth I choose never to marry despite calls from her administrators to do so? In the US: Why did it take almost 100 years before our female human animal was granted a constitutional right to vote? Why was Margaret Sanger's fight for reproductive rights so long and arduous? What were the Comstock laws? Who decided Rosie the Riveter must *live* and why? How did they know she would inspire the way she did? Why did Rosie all but disappear after WWII? How might have our country been different if Rosie never vanished? What truly did the Women's Liberation Movement accomplish? If Walter Mondale had not chosen Geraldine Ferraro as his vice presidential running mate would Mr. Reagan still have become POTUS in 1984? Or at the very least would Mr. Reagan have won by such a staggering margin? Roe V. Wade; what demographic, female or male, really make up the majority of its detractors? Why?

These are all questions for which very logical and scholarly answers have already been provided. History tells us exactly what man wants you to think about them. But when you consider any of these questions, or others, differently than how you have been trained to consider and accept them they become more profound for an entirely different reason.

Go ahead… ask them of yourself. Ask them aloud. Ask them of those around you. Bounce them around in your brain and do not settle for the status-quo. Allow the conversations to begin anew and see where they lead. They may lead you to deduce what I have concluded; History is exactly that… his story and not hers. For to have lent any measure of concrete credence reinforcing the inherent greatness of the female human animal via the written word was to perhaps risk opening what the men in power knew to be the real Pandora's Box (the one resulting in the demise of the perverted world they created). And that… in their eyes… was unacceptable.

Take a moment. What has been said here has been much, but it has not been complicated. To the contrary it has been free of complication; it has all been based upon only the most simple, basic, and therefore truest of observations. They are from the perspective of one who would not deny he is merely one animal observing another. He has observed his fellow human animal has forgotten from whence it came.

-On *Animal*-

Animal; it is a word grossly overused out of context. Within our human world it has become synonymous with describing a person, or persons, engaged in behavior (s) deemed very uncouth or not befitting of a human in the slightest of ways; said behaviors are said to be animalistic.

Animal has become reserved for those of us who commit the most heinous of evils; against either our homogeneity or nature… or both. To be an animal, or animalistic in action, is to be the lowest of low. This is what animal has devolved into within the context of our vastly *evolved* human culture. To be an animal is to be savage AND mindless. Given the context with which we have pigeon-holed animal is it any wonder we refuse to see ourselves as such?

Painting such a drastic distinction between how and why we are different, more to the point *better*, than anything animal satisfies our belief we are, at our core, more than primal, evolutionary stunted creatures who are led through daily existences by mere instinct and/ or happenstance. To state, and believe as fact, any creature not human is only some beast incapable of greatness is not just arrogant, but hubris. This belief... our belief... is, to say the least, very misinformed.

It is easy for us to believe all animals, save for us of course, are simple, basic, unintelligent fur-covered, meat-bag beings destined to wander through their meager existences avoiding death, feeding their bellies and having offspring until they die with not a modicum of what may possibly be referred to as a meaningful life in-between.

It is easy for us to believe this because we largely proclaim animals do not share or indicate many, or any, of the characteristics we deem necessary in order to qualify as anything more than just an animal; we *feel*, we *love*, we *consider*, we *think*, we *know* we are *alive*... in other paraphrased Shakespearean words... we have

To-be-or-not-to-be'd the hell out of our own existence and have therefore erroneously concluded that we Are. We are so very grandiose and self-serving in our assessments of our collective and individual selves. Animals are not hindered by such arrogance and are therefore likely more in tune to what our collective ride on this blue and green planet is all about.

We are different in that we are indifferent. We insist we are complicated biological things who cannot simply live according to nature because living simple is not as simple as it sounds. What suffices for animals cannot suffice for us! We are grand and we are brave and we are clever and we are better! We are ordained by god to have dominion over the entire world! What are we here for if not to strive for more than just being animals?

Animals appear to adhere to the most basic rules of life. We create rules where there should be none. Animals, ironically enough, appear to personify live-and-let-live. We personify quite the opposite. Animals appear to take no more than what is needed or necessary. We take as much as we can.

Animals do not appear to betray each other for the sake of gain or profit. We are common practitioners of such methods. Animals do not appear to kill out of joy or malice; however, there may be that chimpanzee phenomenon, but as no human I know of speaks chimpanzee there is no real way to ascertain what exactly those observed behaviors actually mean. We kill for profit, malice and/ or joy and this is not so very difficult to accept. Animals appear to be the mostly benevolent beings we humans insist we truly are. Once upon a long and primal time ago we probably were, but our *progression* through the ages has given us amnesia.

Grant yourself permission to be challenged. Open your mind. Open your soul. Do not insist you are different than what I have described; for to do so would be to deny that you, like me, have been part of the problem all along.

Man as he currently stands is indeed not an animal; he is less than. For in this male dominated world the only reality that continues to be repeated is calculated death, calculated demise and calculated destruction. Life in general is not held sacred. Resources are not shared. People in need are first shamed then ignored.

Man rapes the planet with no thought of what is to come, or what will be left, for those who will follow him. And through all this the female human animal remains the greatest victim of all; for if She were to reclaim her rightful throne so many, many solutions to the world's ills would be recognized then realized and not just paid superficial patronage.

Life remains simple. Find food. Find shelter. Find immortality; keep the species alive... procreate. The Three Truths apply now as much as they ever have. Erasing what nature has orchestrated is not possible: 1) It is better to co-exist and cooperate than not, 2) Fight only when absolutely necessary, & 3) Kill only when truly defending your life or the lives of those whom you have been entrusted to protect.

The time has arrived to remember what it seems we have collectively forgotten. We are but a very small link in the long DNA chain of the evolution of the world. We are animals who have forgotten and ultimately forsaken how to live simply. We have done so at the expense of practically everything and practically everyone around us.

We are no better than all the other creatures with who we share this blue and green planet. We are animals and there is no harm in that… save for the harm (s) we consciously heap upon ourselves and bequeath upon others. But the best part of this reality is the crash course we have forced upon ourselves can be altered and corrected to the betterment of all beings.

Look. And you will see your closest friend, your family, your neighbor… you will see me, but most importantly you will see you. You are an animal; nothing more nothing less. And you, like me, continue to rely on those beautifully primitive instincts nature instilled within our ancestors all those eons ago; whether you know it or not… whether you want to admit it or not. Where does this all leave us you ask? Well… that indeed is a very good question.

-On How It Has Poisoned Us All-

It is what it is as it always has been. This is it; the way
the world and its societal dynamics seem to always be
explained. It is a succinct doctrine that has been so ingrained
within our collective consciousness that to question it seems
and feels inappropriate; awkward. Just another status-quo
not meant to be challenged let alone considered as a
candidate for an upgrade. Could it be this is the reason we
have only appeared to progress in our so-called societal
evolution?

It is in the most intimate of relationships wherein this
phenomenon of blindness reveals itself most heinously.
Long ago it was written just what were to be the required
criteria for the establishment and solidification of a
successful association… between woman and man that is.

Man's conspiracy of world thievery began with the
distorting of the one message; Be good to each other, Take
care of each other. Not only did man's man-made god

command that man must rule, but man's man-made god included instructions on how to initiate the subjugation of the female human animal.

Make for her a prison. Tell her it is not such as she feels. Call that prison a dwelling. Bestow upon her the authority to rule over this dwelling. Tell her it will be her sacred duty to turn this dwelling into a home. Tell her this home will be where she will ensure her man and her children are kept safe; they will be warm, they will be dry and they will be fed. Tell her this place… this home…will be reserved only for the most important of her kind. Tell her those women who would choose not to fulfill this destiny are usurpers of god's will and betrayers of their children and most egregiously of their men. Tell her this is the way things must be for this is, and has always been, the will of god! And as before…twist, pervert, repeat… twist, pervert, repeat beyond recognition; until the desired outcome is achieved.

Where in the glimpses of our pre-History has it ever been

observed just exactly what were, and are, the human animal's expected roles with regard to gender? Where in the animal kingdom has it been observed the females of any species are, and always have been, subordinate to their respective male counterparts? Where in any aspect of animality has it been observed that females absolutely require males for anything more than reproduction? From where in those minute glimpses of our pre-History does one even begin to profess to have deciphered data leading to *evidence* that males have always been the more dominant of the two? And then not simply to profess unlocking such *knowledge*, but to insist said *knowledge* came from God?!

You may have observed all of the aforementioned questions are rhetorical in nature. That is because you already know the answers. To state, or even suggest, any measure of *evidence* found dating into our pre-History suggests, or implies, the male of any species is the most dominant appears more false than not. I will call it a bald faced lie.

Perhaps it is closer to the actuality of it all to say males of most mammalian species possess the physical attributes necessary to be more domineering than their female counterparts. One who is dominant can be domineering, but one who is domineering is likely not dominant at all and never has been nor shall ever be. Dominant and domineering are not one in the same. They are quite the opposite. And this may most closely define the supreme difference between the female human animal and her less impressive male counterpart. This observation is plain, it is simple and it is just.

The irony here, of course, is this is not how our greater societal dynamics work. The written word as constructed and propagated by man has taught us all what it means to be a man or a woman; each with their own clearly defined gender roles/ expectations; though, these appear to be more readily challenged, weakened, and redefined daily in our contemporary world. But alas even this is all happening at something far, far less than at break-neck speed.

This exercise of caution is likely what man continues to want. For in taking more time than is necessary to bring the world back into its truest natural balance the more time man has to reconnoiter the resistance, plan a response and then execute his next course of action. All this for the probable purpose of *helping* the female human animal feel like she has achieved something akin to equality and should therefore take her foot off the proverbial gas pedal; much like what seems to have occurred in the United States during the Women's Liberation Movement of the 70's.

There is a humor in what has just been said; albeit a sad, biting and ironic humor. The irony is clear to recognize and grasp when one simply chooses to embrace it as nothing more than what it is; the sad and biting part come in when one realizes that deep down inside they, and you, have known it all along. For IT is not a complications-filled concept; just like all of the other observations you have been made privy to so far.

IT is as follows: there is one thing every male human animal shares with all other male human animals. He shares this one thing with them no matter the city, town, province, or country and no matter their politics or their lack thereof of. IT has been constant throughout our time.

IT is the inherent understanding that we, as male human animals, never have been nor shall ever be any kind of real equal to any female human animal. We inherently know we are not in control when it comes to the relationship dynamics between her and us. We inherently know we do not choose her. We inherently know she chooses us or she does not. We inherently know we are powerless in her wake. We inherently know she is power innate. We inherently know we are at her mercy… always. We inherently know we are vulnerable and small when allowed to stand in her light. We inherently know we are her second. We inherently know this is the way things have always been and that THIS will not ever change.

All of the above I will call facts for I am a man and I cannot deny that what is true is true. Any man who argues their veracity is motivated by his own fears, his own inadequacies, and his own selfish misgivings. The world of human animals continues to operate as it does not because the solution to bringing the world back into balance is too complex or indecipherable to find. It continues as it does precisely because the solution is so simple. It is a Hiding-In-Plain-Sight phenomenon we can no longer afford to pretend not see or feel.

Realizing, embracing, and accepting these newly mentioned *truisms* does not make better instantly what seems to have been occurring for a very, very long time now. Recall that it was the birth of agriculture that appears to have begun the demise of our matriarchal nomadic tribes simply being and living simply. At the hands of **domineering** male human animals, now called men, we were devolved into collections of patriarchal clique's overextending their natural parameters. Finite resources were now taken for granted. Patriarchal bullies imposed their physical strengths, amassed and stolen riches and their collective wills upon those they had every intention of subjugating.

That unnatural setting was the moment man ensured the enslavement of the female human animal. He sentenced her to his uncompromising dungeons of societal and gender role expectations. Man's own fears, his own inadequacies and his own selfish misgivings paved the way for his naturally domineering self to crush the spirit of the female human animal. He granted himself license to treat her as something much, much less than what she had always been. The Law of the Three C's (Compassion, Cohesion & Communication) was strangled, mangled, and for all intents and purposes killed. It was replaced by the domineering presence of man whose only goal was to complete the theft of the world; the female human animal's honor, dignity, and nobility be damned!

Take heart. What is and what has been is not necessarily what must continue to be; for we, like all of our animal cousins, possess the instinctual prowess to learn to establish new and improved patterns of behavior. And learn from our mistakes we shall, but first as in all past instances of restoring balance to the natural order of things a reckoning must befall us.

-On the Reckoning-

You have heard it said beauty tames the savage beast. Perhaps you believe man can be soothed by the one woman **he** has chosen to take part in **his** life. Perhaps you feel it is true because in your life you have experienced it this way at one point or another. It is not your fault you may believe and feel as you do. You are not wrong. You are not right. You are misinformed.

Remember that we are all of us animals primarily. As animals we are inherently guided by the purest and most natural of instincts. As such it is no mystery as to why beauty actually does appear to tame the savage beast. She does so not because of any benevolence he feels towards her in the wake of his supposed superiority. She does this precisely because he knows instinctually his place in her presence.

He KNOWS instinctually whose power reigns supreme within the dynamics of the life **she** has chosen to share with him. He KNOWS instinctually his anger and rage originate from a place of personal inadequacy and fear. He KNOWS instinctually when **she** chooses to walk into the tempest of his anger, rage, fear, and personal inadequacy that he looks into the face of God and she is the reason he is no longer afraid.

This is the How and the Why of beauty actually taming the savage beast. It is not that she pleads for him to calm. It is not that she is afraid for herself. It is because she KNOWS his fear, anger, rage, and deeply felt personal insufficiencies are his own worst enemies and she KNOWS she is the one whom is catalyst for him to remember he does not have to be afraid; that all will be well.

All of this is you have felt swimming within you all the days of your life; though perhaps, you could not put your finger on what exactly it was. In all that time you were not overthinking, overreacting or over reaching. In those moments in that time your instincts... your ancestral soul-strings... were talking to you and you just were not sure if you should have listened. The answer then was the same as it is now; yes. Always listen to your soul.

This knowledge has been yours evermore. It is a knowledge that has stirred within you when things with your significant other have been less than ideal. Inside your physical being your gut told you something was off. You were not ill. You were not sad. You were not scared. You were none of these things, but you were unsettled and something did not just *feel* right.

You may have had this unsettled feeling more times than you might want to admit. You may have felt you were just being too sensitive. You may have felt you asked the wrong question or gave the wrong answer. You may have felt you caused another to be hurtful or harmful toward you. You may have felt you deserved it.

That unsettled feeling was, and is, more than what you have considered it to be. It is the voice of God reinforcing the natural instincts so instilled within you from the beginning of your time on this blue and green planet; that voice, those instincts, have tried to warn you when you have not been in situations favorable to your survival- physical or emotional. All animals possess this preservational instinctual knowledge. We have come to refer to this phenomenon as the Fight-or-Fight Response.

It is ironic that of all the creatures on this spinning ball of life we appear to be the one species voluntarily forgoing this Flight-or-Fight Response more often than we choose to employ it. The rub of course is that we are supposed to be intelligent. Yet, we refuse to get out of our own way. Animals in nature live according to The Three Truths and do not ignore their instincts. Perhaps if we did the same we might be less inclined to abjectly embrace the maltreatments of another for any extended amount of time.

All this being said it continues to remain incumbent upon us to decide in which direction we will travel. Will we keep repeating detrimental patterns of choices and behaviors that inexplicably justify the ignoring of deeply ingrained warnings from within our souls or will we choose to be more receptive of what our instincts are trying to tell us?

Changing patterns of choices and behaviors is not difficult. The difficulty lies in being stymied by the fear of what comes with doing almost anything differently. This particular fear is primal for it is the fear of the unknown and it is another ancestral soul-string connecting us back to our very beginning. From our days as *primitive* nomads to our existence as *civilized* peoples today fear was, and is, the cementing force underpinning our collective, misguided belief that stunted and minor progress is progress nonetheless.

Patterns of choices and behaviors are repeated even though they may be detrimental to our being because even in dysfunction it is possible to find comfort. That comfort is predictability. An environment or situation that is predictable can be prepared for and the probable percentages of survivability increased, at the very least mitigated; hence, comfort in discomfort or perhaps more precisely... predictability. Unpredictability is the root of all fear. And fear is the father of all infertile fantasies.

Fear, fear and more fear; there is always more than enough to go around. It is sold to us wholesale on socially grand scales as well on easy to dole out individual serving sizes. It is hard not to choke on at least some of it some of the time. Fear is ubiquitous but it is not omnipotent and like all things it serves a purpose, but its intended purpose is more in line with what we truly are as instinctual animals than what we profess to be and behave like as *intelligent* beings. As well... there is fear legitimate and fear perceived.

Perhaps it was fear perceived and nothing more led to the male human animal's initial misgivings, mistrusts, and misbeliefs he must steal the world from the female human animal in order to ensure his significance. Perhaps it was fear perceived set in motion the disruption of the natural order of things so long ago. Perhaps it is fear perceived continues to perpetuate this disruption today. But fear, whether real or perceived, does not have to hold sway over our collective human animal-ness; and the way things have been does not mean that is the way they must remain.

Fear like all else has its lifespan. The day arrives when its power to cause and to effect wanes. Then soon follows a time when the mist clouding the consciousness lifts. This is difficult to deny; for some sort of reckoning seems to always have its day and ultimately collects its pound of flesh. Balance, it would seem, is universal. The equilibrium of the universe remains uneven only for so long before the balance machine of the cosmos auto-corrects and begins to restore the natural order of things. Evolution is inevitable. This applies in all aspects of life; from our own personal microcosms of existence to the grandiosity of countless universes of which we still have no idea.

The restoration of our world will commence when first and foremost there occurs a shift in our antiquated, collective mind-think. Never was the female human animal meant to be any sort of inferior being to the male human animal. Always was she meant to hold the keys to the kingdom. Our mind-think has for too long negatively reinforced the premise that the way things have been is the way they must have always stood. Through this we have only continued to ensure our ensnarement in the feverish chaos of the now.

It is not that we have found, or continue to find, things impossible to change; it is that we insist their change is improbable and therefore too established to even consider challenging. But this is, and has been, just the fever talking. Do not forget...the theft of the world was MANufactured. Or... perhaps it is more accurate to say the world was manuFRACTURED; nay... for at further dissection still it is clear the world appears to have actually been MAN-

FRACTURED.

This, at the very least, should be enough to illustrate to the masses that if the aforementioned is the way things were always meant to be then somebody made a big, f*#!ing mistake. Evolution is nothing more than life unfolding as it is intended and as is necessary in order for the natural order of things to remain in balance. To hinder or stunt life's progression is to attempt to spit in the face of God. But no matter how ferociously one, or many, may try to usurp the truest intents of life their efforts will always, for them, result in a zero sum game; for LIFE will always find a way *(Thank you Dr. Malcom-Jurassic Park ca. 1993)*.

To be sure there will be those whom will argue, shout, pout, fuss and fight that change is not necessary. *This is the way things are meant to be! It is the way they have always been! There is no reason they should, or must, change! Besides... why should they? So sayeth the Lord!*

Diabolical detractors and deceitful decriers they shall

be... one and all; for theirs will the world coming to an end yet also benefitting the most from this evolution revolution. But to this they will likely be blinded by their own fear, selfish misgivings and personal inadequacies.

Anger will have little to do with their outcries; fear will be their father. For their fear will be born of a perceived belief they will be punished for the sins they have willingly committed and perpetuated against the natural order of things time and time again. But the reckoning that is to come will not be awash in seeking and exacting retribution upon those who participated more fully in the decline of this world. It will not be bloody and it will not be violent; but there shall be some collateral damage all the same.

What will be set to die is our ingrained belief that how things have been is the way things have always stood. A reawakening shall occur and The Three Truths shall be re-embraced. Life will again be simple and balanced as per the natural order of things; even in this modern day world of super-charged technological and scientific wonder.

What we have thus far accomplished on this blue and green spinning ball of life will not have to be relinquished nor torn asunder. In point of this soon to be very real fact… with balance restored greater pinnacles of achievement will be realized at more rapid intervals.

No longer will human animals only hope for solutions to evils once heralded insurmountable. We human animals shall be collectively poised to re-accept our charges as stewards, and not conquerors, of this and other worlds. We shall ultimately save our Mother Earth from ourselves and in turn our Mother will not find it necessary to hold us accountable to the nth degree. And yet none of this will happen unless the female human animal is restored to her rightful throne.

But the one lingering… burning question remains; *How?*

-On the One Burning Question-

It is time to embrace life offers only two choices when it comes to anything and everything that occurs in our lives. Some things knock us sideways; others knock us down... for a while. No matter how heavy life may strike we are never without choices. Many are left to wonder what to do. Many are unsure of how to proceed even if they have some idea of what they can or want to do. Only two things are certain; we can do NOTHING and everything stays exactly the same/ gets worse... OR... we can do SOMETHING and things begin to get better.

It does not take someone more intelligent than I to conclude doing NOTHING pays mostly only the darkest of dividends. Doing SOMETHING, on the other hand, seems to always present us with more options; and that generally brings with it an increased likelihood of more positive outcomes. It is difficult, for me at least, to understand how any one individual, or any one group of individuals, can logically choose not to be proactive when faced with the stark reality that is doing NOTHING vs. doing SOMETHING.

Of course the doing SOMETHING part is completely relative to an individual's circumstance or situation and must therefore fully respect the particular parameters and pieces of those individual life-puzzles. After all, even though our lives may be similar they are not the same. But though our lives are not the same our collective stake is indistinguishable.

What is at stake is not simply the complete restoration of the female human animal's sacredness to her rightful throne, but also the state of our collective being and the health of our planet; for in the hands of man is where the world has been held hostage all these past generations and it is not difficult to know and feel how negatively impactful his domineering grasp has been.

Balance restored is desperately needed. That reckoning

lies cradled within the hands of the female human animal. Our salvation emanates from within her. It always has. If she would but choose to lead… the masses would follow. This reckoning is not for her to request. It is for her to demand! To reclaim outright! To be sure to her reemergence there will be challengers, but those who would seek to deny what is necessary will be choosing to remain shackled to the imagined gilded-ness of the man- domineered past. His grasp upon the world will be no more and in Her hands the world will begin to heal.

This revolution will wholeheartedly reinforce and strengthen all aspects of our collective consciousness in nothing but positive ways. What the female human animal must first re-realize is that she, and only she, is imbued with the inherent soul secrets of Life required to master immortality; she must remember SHE is unequivocally necessary and nothing, or no one, can ever alter that reality no matter how hard they have tried, or are still trying, to snuff the sacredness of her truest essence.

For many a generation man has been successful in convincing the female human animal she is less-than without him and he has displayed his corrupting coup in a disgustingly triumphant manner throughout the ages, but now the time has come for his continued thievery of the world to end.

The restoration of the world is simply about balance. It is ironic this balance will likely appear one-sided through the eyes of those whom do not wish to see the re-birth of the world. To them it shall seem the world will be turning upside down and they may struggle mightily to keep from being swept into a void of misogynistic, masochistic, and mitigated male-dom. But remember, theirs will be a fear unwarranted; for the revolution will not be about their punishment. It will be about liberation… all of ours.

Fear may stymie the ability of some to think rationally for a little while, but alas they too shall awaken. There will be men who will lament the death of their once-upon-a-time; however, this will be dejection unique to the male human animal for he is a creature who thinks, feels, and believes he has reached the pinnacles of his collective natural and metaphysical evolution. The male human animal's life is a life lived for the immediacy of it all with no eye set for the real future; save for the past he seems to collectively wish to re-create. All in all this method of resistance offers no real resistance at all; for always it is consumed by revolution and evolution. What is better naturally always wins out in the end.

And so the one burning question remains: What do we do? I, for one, do not know what you should do. I only know what I shall do. I shall remain silent no more. My actions and my words shall continue to be congruent... every day. Unfairness, indignity, apathy, and cruelty will be met with equal fervor and they shall be made to rue the day they came upon me or allowed me to bear them witness. I am tired of them all. It is a carousel of carnage and all we seem to collectively do is complain over and over and over again. I am tired of watching too many others behave as if nothing can be done about what we all know can be different... nay, better... about OUR blue and green spinning ball of life; about ourselves. I am tired of waiting for the world to come around.

It is time for the female human animal to reclaim her rightful and natural throne and set her sights to the rebalancing of the world.

-On Delving Deeper-

To the extent what I have said has permeated into you please know that it has not been my intention to convince you of one thing or another. My purpose here has not been to get you to agree with me. It has not been about hoping you, or others, will think me right. My purpose has been only to try and show you what has been happening before your eyes; to consider tilting your head just a little that you may see what I have been seeing.

It is not that I believe I am right, wrong, correct, or incorrect for these are subjective concepts. Their determination is really only a matter of assignment and most times that is generally done on a personally biased level. It is that just like you, I know and feel the power that is the inherent recognition of Good from Bad; for this intrinsic principle lives within us. It walks with us from the beginnings of our days, through the darkest and brightest times of our lives, and it is with us until our lives end in what hopefully has culminated in a fulfilling existence void of regrets. This intrinsic power of recognizing Good from Bad is the truest quality of our soul and we are beholden unto it… always.

I have spent many years working with people. They have been children and they have been adults. They had suffered and they were the suffering. They have been the abused and they have been the abuser; sometimes they were both. They were not all the same, but they all seemed to share the same pain… the same sorrow and they all strived to want better.

All these days of being invited into people's lives as they have struggled through very difficult times has provided me with much opportunity to learn something very important and that is: What is and what has been happening **IS** real.

It would be easy to fill the next few pages with my days of adventure, pride, happiness, sadness, anger, frustration, and confusion in all of those emotional and trauma filled trenches, but perhaps it would be better to focus on a few of the most significant things I observed.

1) Girls (especially pre-adolescent girls) are absolutely fearless. They seem to inherently know, accept, and respect their Power. They offer apologies to no one for whom and what they are and their confidence is supreme. They appear to know their lives are filled with infinite choices of which THEY are in total and complete control. 2) Boys (especially pre-adolescent boys) are absolutely accepting of their place as very small particles dancing in the light of a Power that is not their own. They do not question why. They just appear to know this is something not meant to be questioned. It simply is as it should be and it is not a bad thing. 3) Emotional pain and trauma, although relative, are debilitating to all in varying degrees. 4) There is no way around, over, or under emotional pain and trauma; one must choose to walk directly through it in order to get to the other side of their life. 5) The human spirit is indelible and although it can be crushed it can never be truly snuffed; it is absolutely resilient. 6) Girls

(especially adolescent girls) appear to collectively shelve their uber-confident personas of pre-adolescence and begin a process wherein the new self appears to require outside validation; mainly from boys. They appear to relinquish their inherent Power of Being in exchange for an existence of navigating how to be chosen rather than doing the choosing. 7) Boys (especially adolescent boys) appear to collectively sense this change in relational dynamics and begin to play it up for what it is worth. 8) This particular dance, if not course-corrected, continues by and large into adulthood and possibly becomes the foundational setting upon which many, many relationships are built. This is shaky ground to say the least. 9) Women, more often than not, trade pieces of their soul for the sake of creating or preserving "happiness" with a man despite knowing in her core it will not work. 10) Men... all men... inherently know their place in the light of She who is Woman; it is as her subordinate... always.

What is to be said of the above? Is it *right*? Is it *correct*? I do not know. All that can really be said is that the observations were what they were and they are what they continue to be. Of the aforementioned it is number 5 that, to me, is of most meaning for it denotes the one thing that us makes most like each other: The human spirit is indelible and although it can be crushed it can never be truly snuffed - it is absolutely resilient.

Concede you are living a life you feel you were not meant to live. The life you have lived thus far has not been living at all. You wake. You breathe. You will your way through the day, but always you know there is more than a little something missing… from your soul. You are content you say, but this does not necessarily mean you are happy. You want what you know swims in your soul… love, compassion, understanding, & fearlessness. But something else is driving your life and these essential ingredients of what it is to be truly happy remain ever elusive.

Imagine now you are sitting in a car… any car. You are in the backseat. Someone or something shrouded in shadow is in the front. It's black as pitch hands slither like snakes round and round over the steering wheel like witches conjuring curses. The car growls; it is angry. You cannot get out. The doors will not open and the windows will not roll down. Like a bullet you are shot deep into the crevasses of the seat. You go from zero to panic in an instant. Your heart is in your throat.

You yell at the shadow to slow down, but you are ignored. The car screams murderous screams as it lurches back and forth like violence you have known before. Your body crashes against glass and steel. You are a bag of meat trapped in a machine of evil that is pummeling your very soul. You are being tenderized. You are being prepared to be the feast for some beast and all you can do is wait... all you can do is be silent.

Your eyes are pendulums. Your head is a turret. Your

hands are vices cementing you in place. You are being carried to darker and darker places. Ghostly figures roam in and out of the haze glazed night bathed in the dying luminescence of the stars, the moon, and battered street lights. The wind whispers at you through steel and fear is your only friend. You wish upon wish that you wake up… but you are not sleeping.

The car stops as fast as it exploded onto the road. Your eyes struggle to see where you have arrived. It does not matter because it *feels* familiar. You do not know why, but you do not want to be there. You want to leave. You will trade the fright of being trapped in a carriage of carnage if it means you will stop feeling what you are feeling in this moment. It is not fear you feel. It is helplessness. From the backseat you throw fury laden fists at the shadow. He is cold… ice cold… to the touch. You yell. You scream. You cannot be where he has taken you. In a half-circle the shadow head turns and you hear, "I am driving. You go where I take you. You stay as long as I want you to stay."

There is no mouth. There are no eyes. There is only pain.

This is what it is to not be in control of your life. This is
what it is to be afraid every day. This is what it is to have
pain… your pain... be the driving force of your existence.
And pain, as you may very well already know, will have its
way with you… if you allow it.

We have all endured pain. We have all endured strife; and
though some may have indeed felt their only option was not
to go on, many more of us chose to just… keep… moving.
This movement may not have always been in a straight line.
It may have meandered like a wandering river weaving its
way thru life; flowing fast where there was the least
resistance and slowing when the terrain became more
challenging, but never stopping. In those days when we had
chosen to remain steadfast and resilient in spite of the
cumbersome life-terrains we were living we had chosen to
do SOMETHING instead of DOING NOTHING and that

moved us further from the deepest, darkest places of our core and closer to realizing our fullest potentials and greatest senses of self-worth.

Imagine you are back in that car being transported to places, times, and feelings bathed in pain. But imagine now that calm washes over you and for the first time in a long time, or perhaps for the first time ever, you are clear of mind. Your breathing slows. The beating of your blood-pump softens to a harmonic lub, dub… lub, dub… lub, dub. Your eyes are pendulums no more and they are fixed… on the future. Your head is still as a lighthouse in a storm. From that backseat of the car of your life you stretch over the shadow of pain driving your existence and you begin reaching for the keys in the ignition.

You struggle mightily to reach them for pain is not a barrier easily overcome and although it does not fight you it does not willingly get out of your way. Your fingers finally find their prize. You cup the keys in your hand and instantly you are sitting behind the wheel. You caress the keys. In the distant horizon the brilliant sun blooms and breathes a new day. You grip the wheel. You look in the rearview mirror and there… in the backseat…you see it. It is pain…sitting where fear had cemented you in place long ago.

You stare deep into the dead eyes of the all too real pain of your life. Courage finds you and from your heart emanates these words, *"I see you. I will pretend no more that you are not there. You will always be with me. You are me and I am you. We are one. But the time has come for you to take your permanent place in that backseat. I am driving my life now and we shall go where I want to go. We shall remain where I want to remain as long as I want to remain there for you… are in control of my life nevermore!"*

With a clean twist of the keys the engine of the car of your life thunders a guttural growl of defiance and into the dawning of the new life that has always been waiting for you speed headlong.

-On Right Now-

As of this very sentence is has been almost nine years since I began laying the foundations of these words. In point of fact December 27, 2016 will mark nine years exactly. That is the anniversary of Benazir Bhutto's murder. I continue to marvel how the very particular event of her assassination stirred within me the inspiration to speak up and speak out. I was saddened at her demise and I am saddened still at the promise of what may have been her truest potential; for if she could inspire someone on the other side of the world to be silent no more how might she have inspired those in her own country to take a stand?

Nine years is not what is has taken me to complete this work because in truth it has always been finished in my head and in my heart. I have been waiting, but for what I have not really known... until our right now. We are on the cusp of a societal evolution. We are the verge of changing the world most profoundly than ever before. For in the greatest and most powerful nation on our blue and green spinning ball of life there is a changing of the guard set to commence and with it the opportunity to smash an old-world male, dominated order.

It is not for me to say that biology, nor anatomy, make any politician better than another. After all I, on top of being nothing more than someone whose has chosen to view life from an array of angles, am not a political scientist either. What I argue is what I have argued from the beginning of our time together on these pages.

This is the moment wherein the female human animal may begin to reclaim her throne of the world. This is moment wherein many of the atrocities of the past and many of the continued tribulations of the present can be fully and completely acknowledged, stared in the face, and with bravery of soul be smote into submission. This is the moment wherein she may exact her truest strength and stand together as one with all others just like her.

She must do this because right now there is an orange menace about. He is the past fervently clinging to antiquated mind-think hell bent on continuing man's stranglehold upon the world. Many who blindly follow his lead are those who would not see the dawning of a new day because in the dark of the past is where they would choose to remain. They would rather see the world stay exactly the same as it is now, or even take it backwards, because to them these are better alternatives than knowing the world will evolve without them anyway.

In their own twisted and perverted way they champion slavery. They champion injustice. They champion bigotry. But most profoundly they champion against the female human animal and shout profanities about the need for her continued shackled existence. The orange menace and his brethren are the living, breathing embodiments of despair for they are full of fear. And fear must be the last thing allowed to drive our lives ever again. These observations are plain. They are simple. They are fair and they are just. They are that to which the world has been witness and assertions bearing real substance to the contrary would be difficult to argue indeed.

The time has come to return the heir of the world to her rightful throne.

-On Pulling Back the Curtain-

I am a stranger to you. Caution and cynicism should accompany anyone when they have chosen to take any new intellectual journey. All matters are significant, but in matters of great significance reckless abandon is a friend to none; for THAT serves only to leave open the door to missing the point altogether. You should know what I am. You should know my history. You should know me.

I am the last in a line of nine. I am he who is of sisters three and brothers five. I am he was born to parents of poverty. I am he whose mother endured year upon year of martyrdom; sacrificing all of her needs, wants, and desires for the sake of her children. I am he whose father had two families; one *official* and one not. I am he whose father provided for both nonetheless. I am he whom has but one ugly memory of that father. I am he who knows he is lucky to have only one. I am he who knows those before me have many, many more. I am he who was witness to strength and true grit personified. I am he whose mother claimed her birthright and left his father because the drinking and the hitting just ... would ... not... stop. I am he whose mother lived her remaining life in the spirit of No More! I am he whose father reclaimed his soul from the demons within and allowed love to take their place. I am he whose mother and father now live in the sky. I am he who carries them both... now and evermore in his heart and in his soul.

It is in the pictures and movies of past memory that the seeds of what I am trying to share with you were planted. My mother took all of her children and left my father. She did not bargain. She did not negotiate. She did not regret. My mother left him, but my father never left us. For the rest of the life that remained in him he provided and remained ever present in our lives. I do not know all of the bad that occurred between them before my mother chose to remember who and what she had always been. I do not know the man my father was before the demons within poisoned him with their venom. What I know is that when my mother left him and did not return my father's behavior changed… for the better.

For the precious few years they each had left I watched as they treated each other with, what looked and felt like to me as, the utmost respect. When my mother told my father that his children were in need, he always came through. It was funny to sometimes watch him complain because he was a bit of a miser, but never did it seem to me that he regretted doing what was necessary and what was good.

Sundays saw my father walking through the door of whatever house we were then living to take his seat at one end of the table where we all shared breakfast together as a family; my mother always sat at the head opposite of my father. If there was negative discourse or resentment between them I never witnessed or felt it. Nor was I ever made aware of any from my siblings. What I did hear practically every time we were all together was my mother regularly asking my father how he was doing. Was he eating? Was he feeling well? Was his other family taking care of him? My father's quiet demeanor would only allow him to utter that he was fine on all counts. My mother usually finished her round of questions with a statement: *"Por que no te vienes con nosotros? Yo te cuido."* Why don't you come live with us? I'll take care of you.

I never heard my father answer that last question and although I will never know what he may have wanted to say, the one thing I do know is that my mother and my father cared for each other.

They were beautiful. Whatever negativity my mother and my father had shared during their once-upon-a-time appeared to have been swept away into oblivion by the proverbial winds of change set in motion by my mother's bold decision to reclaim her throne. My father, I believe, was proud of her for doing what she did and maybe… just maybe… he was too proud to say so. Perhaps this was why he never answered that last question my mother always asked him every Sunday.

We all got older and Sundays turned into just regular days before the week started again. My mother and my father continued to dance their same beautiful dance whenever they were around each other and their children began to find their own ways through the world. I was the last to leave. At seventeen I hit the road. I did not get to where I was going, but… I did end up, as it turns out, exactly where I was supposed to be.

She had long, blonde hair and her eyes were green emeralds shining through the dim light of the dusty, fluorescent bulbs above. She walked towards the cash register… smiling… her hips swaying slightly this way and that. She put something on the counter and in my sexy, red gas station attendant smock I took it and began ringing her up. Chit chat this… chit chat that…blah, blah, blah… and then she invited me to a party. Almost four years later my baby girl was born and my life became hers.

What is there to say about those almost four years? Well, not much really. Things were good and then they were not. All I will say is that it serves no purpose to vilify or condemn, but that being said I do find it necessary to tell you neither she nor I was ever violent to the other in any way, shape, or form. All that mattered to me from that point was encased in a chubby, baby girl with marshmallowy feet, hazel-green, brown eyes, & curly, curly brown hair.

For what turned out to be very near eight years my daughter's mother and I had an exceptional, professional co-parenting relationship. Whereas she worked days, I worked swings. Everyday my baby girl and I would be together until it was time for me to start my work. We were together every weekend too. It was not a matter of forced visitation, you see. It was simply a matter of me not caring to behave like I was single and carefree. I just wanted to be with my little girl and I did not care if that meant all week, all weekend… every weekend. Life was simply beautiful and good. It was me and her against the world.

My daughter was nine when it started. It happened in the parking lot of her school. The teacher conference had gone well and I was getting ready to leave. My daughter's mother came to me and said she needed to talk. She wanted tell me that she had decided to start a new and serious relationship. I congratulated her and told her I was happy for her. I truly was. But the words that fell out of her mouth next were cause for much, much concern.

She told me that all matters regarding my daughter would now be required to go through her new boyfriend. She said visitation schedules would now have to be put in place and no longer would we be so fluid with the way we had been raising our daughter. Confusion took hold of me and then anger began to simmer within. I could not believe what I was hearing. For the whole of my baby girl's life her mother and I had done well being civil and respectful of one another and now things, it seemed, were poised to change for my little

girl… and not for the best. Confusion and the anger quickly

faded and astonishment set in. Astonished. Yes, that is what

I was feeling. Astonished.

Having already spent what was soon to be my first

decade working with emotionally injured people, I knew in

my heart the origins of her proclamations. Fear, fear, and

more fear. I asked my daughter's mother if she was ok. She

said yes. I repeated her words because I wanted to be certain

I heard them entirely. I had. I asked her if she was serious.

She said she was. To her revelations I could only say but one

thing; No. Worry washed across her face as if she was

envisioning what might happen later when she would have

to tell her new beau I was not going to play their game. She

told me to expect to hear from the Court. I said I would.

Three years later after putting up much fight and after

having time with my little girl slowly eroded away to three

weekends a month the Court allowed the woman that gave

birth to my daughter to take her 200 miles away from me. There is another, entirely engrossing story here that clearly paints the picture of what happened, but again… to vilify or condemn serves no purpose. My daughter and I had gone from being together practically every day of her entire life, to having three weekends together, to now being relegated to seeing each other for what would turn out to be roughly thirty-six hours every other weekend. Those were the longest and hardest two years of my life.

For seven hundred-thirty days I was an exposed nerve. My days flooded with thoughts of, "just… keep… moving." Do stuff… any stuff… in the morning until it was time to go to work. Go to work. Finish work late at night. Go do something else until exhaustion lived in my bones. Go home. Lay my head down only to be awake… all over again; worries about my little girl creeping and crawling like maggots in my head…eating holes in my heart. Waiting and waiting for the every other weekend to come. It… never coming fast enough.

Drive 4 hours to get her. Drive 4 hours back. Race to see family. Race to spend time together. Hold my tongue about now much I want her to come home. She looks and acts like she is ok. For thirty-six hours I do not have to worry. I do not have to just... keep... moving. I can sleep. The time...it is gone... again. Drive 4 dread filled hours to take her back. Drive 4 dread filled hours back without her... I am alone... I am all alone. The clock starts over. Two weeks to go. Two weeks more of just... keep... moving; I feel heavy and drenched in sorrow like a stone at the bottom of the sea. *"It will all be ok,"* I tell myself. *"It really will."*

In my heart I carry one thing. *"She will be back. The pieces of the puzzle she cannot see right now will fall into place and she will be back."* More Court... more attempts to keep stealing more time away... there is fight left in me still. I will never stop fighting. She is my daughter and she will at least know that I tried and I tried and I tried.

Finally… it comes; the day she says, *"Daddy, I want to come home with you."* She is fourteen… just starting high school. I ask her if she is sure. She says she is. I tell her I have to follow the rules. I tell her I will start tomorrow. She says ok. This day… this drive is not filled with dread… I do not feel alone. This day… I am happy for the first time in two years.

4 hours later I am home. My little girl calls. She says, *"Daddy, can I come home tomorrow?"* My heart climbs up into my throat and steals the wind from my voice. I want say yes, but I can't. I have to follow the rules…. the rules of the Court. *"I have to go through the Court, Mama."* My baby begins to cry. *"Daddy, I don't want to be here anymore."* I ask her if she has spoken to her mother. She says yes. I ask her what her mother has said. *"She says she just wants me to be happy."* From my heart comes pouring, *"I'll be there tomorrow."* I tell my baby girl I love her. She says, *"I love you too."*

The next morning… up before the sun. 4 hours later the school is in sight. I go in. *"I'm here to withdraw my daughter. She doesn't want to be here anymore. I'm taking her home."* The flunky at the front desk spits some jazz about needing to get the principal. They leave and minutes later dude shows up asking me questions. I hear none of them. He might as well be Charlie Brown's teacher. *"I'm here to take my daughter home. I have joint-custody of her. She does not want to be here."* Whock-Whock vomits a half-hearted attempt at citing the law. He has no idea what is about to hit him. He is an idiot.

"I know this law better than you think you do. I am my daughter's legal guardian. She does not want to be here anymore and so she won't. Call whomever you feel you need to call, but I'm telling you… I'm taking her out of here and you are not going to stop me." In my face he sees what I feel: Conviction. There is nothing he can or should do and he knows it. More minutes pass. Here comes my little girl. We

embrace. We cry. We leave… and just like that it is me and her against the world again.

The days sailed by faster than I wanted. I imagine it is the lament of all parents who love their children dearly, but together my daughter and I remained, nonetheless, through every achievement, every milestone, every sadness, and every happiness of her most important adolescent years. Until, of course, the day arrived when she did as I had done so many years before and struck out on her own… with a daughter of her own.

And so once again I bear witness to purest strength of soul and true grit personified.

-Epilogue-

It is true I am really no one academically qualified to espouse what I have been sharing. It is true the extent of what most certainly should not even loosely be referred to as *my research* is grounded simply in the observing of the actions and reactions of others. It is true the near twenty-five years I spent working in social services has biased me. It is true what I have observed has remained constant throughout that time no matter the arena of observation. It is also true I have an agenda; for whom among us does not? That agenda is to leave this world better that what I have observed it to be for my granddaughter and my daughter.

What is most true is that I have faith this world... OUR blue and green spinning ball of life... can be more than what we have allowed. We are all in this together. We must remember this always and we must all have faith... in each other. Yet, only one half of us possess inherently the will of the natural order of things. Only one half of us can truly spark the revolution necessary to ensure our salvation and it is time she remembered who and what she has been since the beginning of our ancestors.

Everything begins from within. The smallest of changes initiates the greatest of evolutions and that is fact irrefutable. What is now is not what should have always been, but then again every bit of everything I have offered comes from a place of accepting that I may be branded a simple fool. I possess neither the intellect nor the academic training to insist anything I have said carries any sort of *real* weight, but… this does not mean what I have said bears no substance.

There is one reason and one reason only for what I have tried to give to you; faith.

Where There Is Light

I have faith.

I have faith people will do better despite seeing and hearing
  them at their worst.

I have faith I will be seen as a fool for doing so.

I have faith I will not care if I am a fool.

I have faith in the power of my pen.

I have faith my ink well will not ever run dry

For it is filled with the sweat, blood, and breath

That is conviction undeniable. I have faith

What my eyes see and what my ears hear now, WILL NOT
  be the past

I have read of in the not so long ago Once-Upon-A-Time.

I have faith we will all remember the one thing…

Be Good to Each Other, Take Care of Each Other.

I have faith this will all be ok.

I have faith it really will.

I have faith you will not falter.

I have faith you will not allow others to fall.

I have faith the world is watching and feeling… everything.

I have faith we will all finally listen.

I have faith we will not succumb to fear.

I have faith the world is finally changing for the better.

I have faith the others are scared

    To their core,

Like children drenched in imagined deepest, darkness.

I have faith they will learn their heart belongs

                in the middle

                of their soul

And not in their throat…

    Where it has been choking them.

I have faith we will all walk with wisdom

                        In the end.

I have faith.

FINI

Original Title

<u>The Theory of Revolution: A Sure Fire Way of Saving the
World In Spite of Man's Best Efforts to Utterly Destroy all
Vestiges of Hope OR… Rosie the Riveter was Right!</u>

Made in the USA
Middletown, DE
08 November 2021

51834725R00096